Victor's Secret

Elizabeth Neblett

PEARSON
Longman

Modern Dramas 3: Victor's Secret
First Edition

Copyright © 2008

Pearson Education, Inc.
10 Bank Street, White Plains, NY 10606

Staff credits: The people who made up the *Modern Dramas 3: Victor's Secret* team, representing editorial, production, design, and manufacturing, include Pietro Alongi, Andrea Bryant, Dave Dickey, Ann France, Laura Le Dréan, Martha McGaughey, Jaime Lieber, Michael Mone, and Edie Pullman.

Cover illustration: Seitu Hayden
Text design: Jimmie Young, Tolman Creek Design
Text composition: S4 Carlisle Publishing Services
Text font: 12.5/13 Minion
Illustrations: Seitu Hayden

ISBN-13: 978-0-13-235530-8
ISBN-10:   0-13-235530-2

LONGMAN ON THE **WEB**

Pearsonlongman.com offers online resources for teachers and students. Access our Companion Websites, our online catalog, and our local offices around the world.

Visit us at **www.pearsonlongman.com**.

Printed in the United States of America
4 5 6 7 8 9 10 V063 13 12

Contents

To the Teacher

Victor's Secret is the third book in the series of four Longman *Modern Dramas*. These dramas provide authentic, level-appropriate, engaging literature for adult English language learners. The individual episodes of the books can either stand alone or be taught in sequence as part of an ongoing course. *Modern Dramas* fill the need in the beginning to low-intermediate classroom for controlled reading material of more than a few paragraphs. *Modern Dramas* also keep the students interested in what they are reading: They will want to keep turning the pages to find out what happens next.

You will be amazed at how engaged your students will be with these stories. The involving story lines will draw students in and motivate them to keep on reading. The language is not completely grammatically controlled; *Modern Dramas* aim above all to be interesting and natural and have been written with an eye to research that shows that most students' reading ability is at a higher level than their speaking, listening, or writing skills. By the last episode, your students will be able to follow the plot and to answer the reading comprehension questions without using their dictionaries.

In this third book of the series, ten episodes follow the story of Victor Santos as he strives to balance work and family. Victor has something to hide: he's decided to go back to school for the diploma he never got years ago, and he doesn't want his family to know about it! Students learn vocabulary related to daily-life skills and issues, especially education and employment.

Each of the ten episodes consists of:

- **The opening page**
  A picture sparks student interest in the episode to come and provides a springboard for lively student discussion.

- **Get Ready to Read**
  Three questions directly following the opening art can be discussed in pairs, small groups, or with the whole class. These questions focus students' attention on the theme of the episode. A matching exercise after these questions introduces new vocabulary.

- **In the last episode . . .**
  Each episode starts with a brief summary of the previous episode so that students who were absent will be able to follow the story and students who have been in class will be reminded of what has already happened.

- **The reading**
  Each reading is between 600 and 1,000 words. You can assign the episode and the exercises following it for homework, but it is also useful to read it aloud to the class, or to have the students listen to the recording of the episode before they read it on their own. New vocabulary not targeted on the opening page is defined either with call-out art or with a gloss on the relevant page.

- **Reading Comprehension**
  These true/false and multiple choice questions check students' understanding of what they have just read. The exercises can be used for class discussion. You can encourage students to explain their answers or tell the class where in the episode they found the information to answer the questions.

- **Work with the Words**
  These exercises review and solidify students' knowledge of new vocabulary, both the words targeted on the opening page and other vocabulary words which have come up in the reading. The exercises are multiple choice, fill in the blank, and select the opposite word, among others.

- **Lifeskill Practice**
  These exercises focus on a particular theme or competency featured in the episode. The exercises reinforce standard life skills and competencies.

- **Dialogue Practice**
  Selected portions of the episode are reproduced at the end of each of the ten segments so that students can practice the language in a focused way. These can be used for pronunciation practice or role play.

After your students finish *Victor's Secret*, they will be eager to read the other books in the *Modern Dramas* series: *Solomon the Superintendent*, *Lucy and the Piano Player*, and *Ramona's Adventure*.

The Interview

Get Ready to Read

A Discuss with a partner.

1. Where do you think the man is going?
2. Why is he looking at his watch?
3. What questions do employers ask at job interviews?

B Match the words with the definitions.

_d_ 1. grown
____ 2. promotion
____ 3. rush hour
____ 4. pull over
____ 5. encourage
____ 6. in charge of
____ 7. requirements

a. busy time on the roads, especially morning and evening

b. supervise or manage

c. drive to the side of the road

d. adult

e. give someone confidence to do something

f. things that you have to have before you get a job

g. a change to a better job in the same company, usually with more money

About Victor

Victor Santos lives in Maplewood, New Jersey, with his wife, Marisa, and his two children, Alexandra and Jordan. They are very busy. Next year, Alexandra is going to start college, so Victor is working a lot of overtime to save money. Marisa sometimes works late, too. They are **fortunate** because Victor's mother lives nearby, and she can stay with Jordan when Victor and Marisa have to work late and Alexandra has an after-school activity.

Victor is not happy with the job that he has now, so he is applying for a **promotion** to a better position at the same company.

Marisa is standing at the kitchen door of her home. She's talking to her husband, Victor. "Good-bye, sweetie. See you tonight."

"Thanks, honey. Wish me luck."

"I know that you're going to get that job. I'm going to make a special dinner for you tonight."

"See you later, Marisa."

Victor Santos kisses his wife and leaves for work. When he leaves, Marisa looks out the window to make sure that he's in his car, and then she makes a phone call.

"Luisa? Hi, it's Marisa. Victor is on his way to work. I'm going to come home early to start cooking. Can you come early to help me? What? I know, Victor doesn't have the **promotion** yet, but everyone is sure that he's going to get it. His supervisor gave him a really good recommendation. Yes. Yes. I'm sure it's a good idea to surprise him."

It's the morning **rush hour** on Route 22. The traffic is unusually heavy, so Victor changes the radio station to listen to the traffic report. "Maybe there's an accident," he thinks.

"Traffic is slow on westbound Route 22. There was an accident an hour ago, and the **tow truck** is just now moving a car from behind that **overturned** tractor trailer. The right lane is **blocked**, so give yourself some extra time this morning."

After Victor listens to the traffic report, he looks at his watch. It's 8:15. "I'm going to be late!" he says to himself.

Victor is nervous about his appointment with the manager of Human Resources at nine o'clock this morning. He doesn't talk to the manager often. If there are any problems at work, Victor always talks to his supervisor.

Victor works in the mailroom of TabLet Pharmaceuticals. He has worked there for fifteen years, and he's a little **bored**.* Every day, it's the same thing: read the addresses on the envelopes, put the mail into bags, deliver the mail to offices. The salary and the benefits are good, but Victor wants something more interesting. Last month, Victor applied for a new job at the company. There's a job opening for a supervisor in the mailroom. The current supervisor, Anthony, is planning to retire next month. Anthony likes Victor and thinks that he is a good worker. He **encouraged** Victor to apply for the job. He said, "Victor, I think this is a good opportunity for you. You are one of the best workers in the mailroom. Everybody likes working with you. Apply for the job."

The job of supervisor is more interesting than the job that Victor has now. The supervisor is **in charge of** 20 people. The salary and the benefits are better. If Victor gets the job, he will have two more personal days, two more sick days, and three weeks of vacation every year. He has two weeks now.

Victor **pulls over** to the side of the road. He turns on his cell phone and calls Mr. Stevenson, the manager of Human Resources.

"Human Resources. May I help you?" says the receptionist.

"Yes, may I speak to Mr. Stevenson?" asks Victor.

"Who's calling?"

"This is Victor Santos. I have an appointment with Mr. Stevenson at nine o'clock."

"Just a minute, please."

Mr. Stevenson comes to the phone and says, "John Stevenson speaking."

"Mr. Stevenson, this is Victor Santos."

"Hello, Victor. We have an appointment this morning. Is there a problem?"

"Well, I think I'm going to be late for our appointment. Traffic is terrible because there's an accident, and the road is very slow."

"That's not a problem, Victor. Call me when you arrive. Maybe I can meet you at lunchtime."

*bored = not interested

"Thank you very much, Mr. Stevenson. I'm very sorry. I'll call you again when I arrive."

"You're welcome."

"Good-bye, Mr. Stevenson."

Victor relaxes and gets back on the highway.

*   *   *   *

It's twelve o'clock, and Victor is sitting in Mr. Stevenson's office.

"Well, Victor, your supervisor says very nice things about you."

"That's nice to hear," says Victor.

"He says that you are an excellent employee. You're always on time, you're never late, and he never has to tell you what to do. You always do your work, and everyone likes working with you."

"Thank you," says Victor.

"Victor," says Mr. Stevenson, "did you read all of the **requirements** for this position?"

"Yes, I'm sure I read everything."

"Well, something is missing on your application. This position requires a high school diploma, but I didn't see that on your **résumé**.* Did you forget to write down that information?"

Victor's smile goes away. "No, I didn't forget. I don't have a diploma."

"Do you have a **GED**?"** asks Mr. Stevenson.

"No, I don't," answers Victor. "I don't have a diploma or a GED, but I have fifteen years of experience."

"Yes, I understand that, Victor. But, you see, this position requires a minimum of a high school diploma. I thought you forgot to write it on the

---

***résumé** = your education and work history; curriculum vitae (CV)

****GED** = a graduate equivalency diploma

application. Without a diploma or a GED, we cannot consider you for this position. I'm very sorry. We cannot hire you for this position."

"But, Mr. Stevenson, I'm qualified. I have experience and all of the other **qualifications*** on the job description."

"That's true, and I know you are disappointed, Victor. You are a good employee, and I wish I could give you this promotion, but I'm very sorry. I cannot break the rules. We cannot promote you without a high school diploma or GED. You're a smart man, Victor. Get your diploma. You can apply again."

Victor leaves Human Resources. He thinks, "What am I going to tell Marisa?"

Reading Comprehension

A Circle *True* or *False*.

1. Victor's wife thinks he is going to get the job.	True False
2. Traffic is heavy.	True False
3. Victor listened to a traffic report before he left home.	True False
4. Victor has a car accident.	True False
5. In the car, Victor has a positive feeling about the interview.	True False
6. Victor's job is easy and interesting.	True False
7. Victor wants a more interesting job.	True False
8. The manager of Human Resources is angry that Victor is late.	True False

B Circle the correct answer.

1. Victor thinks that his job is _____.
   a. interesting
   b. boring
   c. exciting
   d. heavy

*qualifications = experience you need for a particular job

2. Victor _____ every day.
   a. opens envelopes
   b. sorts and delivers mail
   c. writes letters
   d. supervises employees

3. Victor calls Mr. Stevenson because _____.
   a. he wants to make an appointment
   b. he wants to cancel the appointment
   c. he wants to change his appointment to an earlier time
   d. he wants to change his appointment to a later time

4. Victor meets Mr. Stevenson _____.
   a. later on the same day
   b. at the same time the next day
   c. in the evening after he finishes work
   d. thirty minutes later

C **Answer the questions.**

1. Why did Victor ask his wife to wish him luck? _____

   _____

2. How long has Victor worked at TabLet? _____

3. What position is he applying for? _____

4. What are the benefits of the new position?
   a. more personal days
   b. more sick days
   c. of vacation

5. What is a serious problem for Victor?
   He doesn't have a _____.

Work with the Words

A Circle the correct answer.

1. I was **fortunate** to find an apartment in this neighborhood. This neighborhood is _____.
   a. very popular
   b. dangerous
   c. not a good place to live
   d. not good for children

2. She received a **promotion** because her boss liked _____.
   a. the mistakes on all of her reports
   b. her clean desk
   c. her attitude and work habits
   d. the many absences from work

3. During **rush hour**, many people _____.
   a. eat lunch
   b. hurry to the bank
   c. take breaks from work
   d. go to work or return home from work

4. The students were **bored** because the class _____.
   a. was very interesting
   b. was fun
   c. was not interesting
   d. had many exciting things to do

5. My parents **encouraged** me to go to college. They said, _____.
   a. "You should go to college. You're a good student."
   b. "Get a job. We don't have money for college."
   c. "College is not important."
   d. "We didn't go to college. It's not necessary for you either."

6. The _____ is **in charge of** the class.
   a. student
   b. teacher
   c. principal
   d. parent

7. I was driving too fast, so a _____ told me to **pull over**.
   a. phone call
   b. driver
   c. police officer
   d. teacher

8. I have the **qualifications** for this job. I have _____.

    a. no experience

    b. a uniform

    c. many friends at work

    d. a high school diploma and some experience

9. My **résumé** includes _____.

    a. the name of my elementary school

    b. my work history

    c. my hobbies and my favorite TV programs

    d. a health evaluation from my doctor

B Complete the paragraphs with the correct words and phrases. You will not use all the words.

bored	GED	pull over	résumé
encouraged	in charge of	qualifications	rush hour
fortunate	promotion	requirement	

1. Victor is usually on time for his appointments, but today he is going to be late. Traffic is always heavy at _____, and there was an accident. He called Human Resources to change his appointment. He was _____ because the manager changed the appointment.

2. Victor is _____ at work. He is tired of doing the same thing every day. He thinks that he has all of the _____ for a _____ to supervisor. Anthony, Victor's supervisor, _____ Victor to apply for the promotion. The supervisor is _____ other employees.

3. There was a problem at the interview. Victor's _____ doesn't list a high school diploma or a _____. A high school diploma is a _____ for the job.

Lifeskill Practice

■ It's useful to be able to talk about traffic problems.

A Practice the conversations with a partner.

1. **Police officer:** Please **pull over**.
   Driver: Is there anything wrong, Officer?
   Police officer: You were driving too fast. May I have your license and registration, please?
   Driver: Of course.

2. **A:** Where's your car?
   B: I parked in a handicapped space. A tow truck took it away. Now I have to pay a big fine.
   A: Too bad.

3. **A:** Traffic is really slow. We're going to be late.
   B: There's nothing I can do. The right lane is **blocked**.
   A: Why?
   B: The traffic report says that there is an **overturned** truck.

B Pairs. Tell your partner about a driving problem you had. Try to use some of the words from Exercise A. Take turns.

Dialogue Practice

Practice the conversation with two classmates.

Receptionist: Human Resources. May I help you?

Victor: Yes, may I speak to Mr. Stevenson?

Receptionist: Who's calling?

Victor: This is Victor Santos. I have an appointment with Mr. Stevenson at nine o'clock.

Receptionist: Just a minute, please.

Mr. Stevenson: John Stevenson speaking.

Victor: Mr. Stevenson, this is Victor Santos.

Mr. Stevenson: Hello, Victor. We have an appointment this morning. Is there a problem?

Victor: Well, I think I'm going to be late for our appointment. Traffic is terrible because there's an accident, and the road is very slow.

Mr. Stevenson: That's not a problem, Victor. Call me when you arrive. Maybe I can meet you at lunchtime.

Victor: Thank you very much, Mr. Stevenson. I'm very sorry. I'll call you again when I arrive.

Mr. Stevenson: You're welcome.

Victor: Good-bye, Mr. Stevenson.

A Decision

Get Ready to Read

A Discuss with a partner.

1. Victor is depressed after his interview. What is he going to do next?
2. Who is Victor going to talk to about his interview?
3. Tell your partner about a job interview you had.

B Match the words with the definitions.

__c__ 1. depend on   **a.** feel thankful

_____ 2. a gossip   **b.** leave school early; not graduate

_____ 3. overhear   **c.** need someone or something

_____ 4. relieved   **d.** stop employing workers, usually because
                              business is bad
_____ 5. appreciate

_____ 6. drop out of   **e.** someone who talks about other people

_____ 7. lay off   **f.** a good feeling after something bad is
                              finished

                         g. hear someone else's conversation

In the last episode...

Victor is depressed. He had an interview at lunchtime with
Mr. Stevenson, the manager of Human Resources at TabLet
Pharmaceuticals. Victor wanted a promotion; he wanted to be a
supervisor in the mailroom, and he has fifteen years of experience.
Mr. Stevenson didn't give Victor the job because Victor doesn't have a
high school diploma.

🎧 Victor is leaving Mr. Stevenson's office in Human Resources. He's talking to himself, "I know I don't have a high school diploma, but I'm an excellent employee. What am I going to tell my family? They're depending on me."

Victor goes down to the mailroom and changes into his uniform. He goes to his regular place and starts working. He doesn't want anyone to know about his interview, so he doesn't say anything about it. Then he sees Mac, his best friend at work. Mac is smiling, and he greets Victor.

"Hey, Victor! **What's up*** with you? You look terrible, man!"

Victor tries to look normal. "I didn't sleep well last night. I'm tired."

Mac looks around to make sure no one is looking, and he whispers to Victor, "**How did it go**?" **

Victor looks surprised. "You know about my interview? How did you know? I didn't tell anybody."

Mac says, "Mercedes, that secretary from **HR**† was in the cafeteria. You know her, Victor. She's the office **gossip**. She knows everything and talks to everyone in the office. I was getting a cup of coffee, and she was talking to her friends. She has a loud voice, and I **overheard** her."

Victor looks **relieved**. He's glad to talk about it with someone. "I didn't get the job."

"What? **Are you kidding?**†† Why not? You're one of the best employees in this department. Everybody here knows that Anthony is going to retire soon. I

***What's up** = a casual greeting: How are you?

****How did it go?** = How was it?

†**HR** = Human Resources

††**Are you kidding?** = Are you telling the truth?

think everybody expects you to be the new supervisor. You have the most experience and everyone likes you."

"Thanks, Mac. I **appreciate** your support, but there's nothing I can do about it."

"What do you mean? Did they hire somebody's relative? A cousin? A nephew?"

Victor laughs. "I don't think anyone has the job yet. I didn't get the job because the company requires a high school diploma for the job. I don't have a high school diploma."

"How about a GED?"

"Nope. I don't have that either."

"Is that the only reason that you didn't get the job?"

"I think so. That's what Mr. Stevenson told me. Anthony gave me a good recommendation."

Mac is shaking his head. "Victor, you're a smart guy. Why didn't you get your diploma? I know you're smart. You help me with my taxes every year."

Victor answers, "I know, but when I was younger, my family had a lot of problems. When my parents came to this country from Brazil, I was only 15, and my sisters were still in elementary school. My father didn't know any English, but he got a construction job through a friend. One day, he was working on a building, and there was an accident. My father didn't have any health insurance, and he couldn't work for a long time. My mother could only work part-time because my sisters were so young—my parents didn't have enough money for childcare, and we didn't have any close family here. I learned English quickly, so when I turned 16, I **dropped out of** school to help my family. We really needed the money. My father started working again a year later, but after I started making money, I forgot about school. I never went back to finish. Now, I have my own kids to think about."

"Wow, you never told me that," says Mac.

"I don't like to talk about it," says Victor.

Then Mac suggests, "Well, what are you waiting for? Go back to school now."

"Are you crazy? I'm over 40 years old. It's too late for me."

"No, it isn't. Many adults get their GEDs. The people in those classes are all different ages. Besides, I heard from Mercedes that TabLet is going to **lay off** ten people next week. This is a good time to get that diploma. It will give you more job security, and maybe you can apply for a promotion in another department," says Mac.

Victor isn't sure. He says, "I don't know. If I go back, I think I would like to get a regular diploma, not a GED. I was a pretty good student in high school, especially in math and English."

"How are you going to get a regular diploma? Do you want to sit in a classroom with teenagers? Your daughter's a high school student. And how are you going to work every day?"

"I don't know, but I'll think of something. Maybe I'll tell my family that I'm working extra overtime or something so I can get some time to study. I need that diploma. But Mac, I have a bigger problem right now. Everybody in my family knows about my interview today. They're expecting good news. How am I going to tell them that I didn't get the job?"

Mac doesn't have an answer.

Later that day, Victor is driving home. Traffic is heavy again, but Victor is glad to have the time alone. He needs to think. He needs to make a decision. "How can I get a diploma? How long will it take?" His cell phone is ringing, but he doesn't answer it. It's his wife, Marisa, again. She is calling to find out about the promotion, but Victor isn't ready to talk about it with her. Victor almost has an accident because he is not paying attention to the traffic; he's thinking about his family. "What is Marisa going to say?"

When Victor gets near his house, he sees a lot of cars on the street. All the lights are on in his house. His father-in-law's car is in front of the house. His sister and her husband's car is in the driveway. Another sister's motorcycle is next to the house. He parks his car across the street and quietly walks up to the back door. "**What's going on?**"* wonders Victor.

* **What's going on?** = What's happening?

Reading Comprehension

A   Circle *True* or *False*.

1. Victor is happy about his interview.	**True**	**False**
2. Victor wanted to change departments.	**True**	**False**
3. Mr. Stevenson told Mac about Victor's interview.	**True**	**False**
4. Mercedes talks a lot about other people.	**True**	**False**
5. Victor feels better after he talks to Mac.	**True**	**False**
6. Mac is surprised that Victor doesn't have a diploma.	**True**	**False**
7. Victor was born in the United States.	**True**	**False**
8. Victor thinks he is too old to go back to school.	**True**	**False**

B   Circle the correct answer.

1. _____ can get GEDs.
   a. Adults
   b. Young people
   c. Women
   d. all of the above

2. Victor is worried about _____.
   a. his parents
   b. his family's reaction to the news
   c. his new responsibilities
   d. Mercedes and her friends

3. In high school, Victor was _____.
   a. a poor student
   b. a good student
   c. the worst student
   d. the most intelligent student

4. Why is this a good time for Victor to get a diploma?
   a. Because he has vacation time
   b. Because he lost his job
   c. Because ten people are going to lose their jobs
   d. Because there's a new GED class

C Answer the questions.

1. How did Mac find out about Victor's interview?

   _____

2. Why does Mac think that Victor is smart?

   _____

3. How did Victor feel on the way home from work?

   _____

4. Who is at Victor's house when he gets home?

   _____

Work with the Words

A Circle the correct answer.

1. Most children **depend on** their _____ to take care of them when they are sick.
   - **a.** school principals
   - **b.** parents
   - **c.** friends
   - **d.** neighbors

2. Nancy is a **gossip**. She likes to _____.
   - **a.** cook
   - **b.** exercise
   - **c.** travel with friends
   - **d.** talk about other people

3. I was in the post office when I **overheard** _____.
   - **a.** a car crash
   - **b.** people complaining about the new price of stamps
   - **c.** a dog
   - **d.** my cell phone ringing

4. The student was **relieved** after he received his exam results because _____.
   - **a.** his grade was poor
   - **b.** his grade was better than he expected
   - **c.** he failed the exam
   - **d.** he failed the course

5. The manager **appreciates** the _____ of her employees.
   a. absences
   b. long coffee breaks
   c. hard work
   d. laziness

6. The factory is going to **lay off** workers because _____.
   a. the company is very successful
   b. the company needs more workers
   c. the company is selling many products
   d. the company's sales are low

7. **A:** What's up?

   B: _____
   a. An airplane.
   b. How are you?
   c. Nothing much.
   d. Fine, thank you.

8. **A:** How did your driving test go?

   B: _____
   a. I drove on the highway.
   b. I passed the first time!
   c. I went home.
   d. Forty minutes.

9. **A:** _____

   B: Are you kidding?
   a. It's a nice day today.
   b. My wife is going to have triplets!
   c. I'm enjoying my class.
   d. I have a bad cold.

B Complete the conversations with the correct words and phrases.

appreciate	gossip	overheard
depend on	How did it go?	relieved
drop out of	laid off	What's going on?

1. **A:** What's wrong?

   B: My company _____ 100 employees today.

2. **A:** I had a job interview today.

   B: _____

   A: I think it went well.

3. **A:** How's your daughter?

   B: We're very _____. She's much better, and she can leave the hospital tomorrow.

   A: That's great!

4. **A:** Did you know that Mario is leaving the company?

   B: How do you know that?

   A: Frank told me, but he's a _____. I don't know if it's true.

5. **A:** I need some help getting ready for the party.

   B: You can _____ me. I'll bring a dessert and some drinks.

   A: Thank you. I _____ your help.

6. **A:** Did you know that the cost of the subway is going up again?

   B: How do you know?

   A: I _____ some transportation workers talking.

7. **A:** _____ You look very happy today.

   B: I got a promotion.

8. **A:** What's wrong?

   B: My daughter wants to _____ college. I'm very disappointed.

Lifeskill Practice

Talking about layoffs

lay off	My company is going to **lay off** 100 employees.
get laid off	I **got laid off** because I was a new employee.
layoffs	There were a lot of **layoffs** last year in my state.

Pairs. Practice the conversations with a classmate.

1. **A:** What's up? You look upset.
   B: I heard that the company is going to **lay off** some people.
   A: Really? Why?
   B: Sales are down.

2. **A:** The company **laid off** 200 workers. What are you going to do?
   B: I'm going to the unemployment office.
   A: Why?
   B: Because I need money, and they can help me find another job.

3. **A:** I have some bad news. There are going to be some **layoffs** in this department.
   B: But I have ten years experience here.
   A: I know. You don't have to worry.

Dialogue Practice

Practice the conversation with a classmate.

Mac: Hey, Victor! What's up with you? You look terrible, man!

Victor: I didn't sleep well last night. I'm tired.

Mac: *(whispers)* How did it go?

Victor: *(surprised)* You know about my interview? How did you know? I didn't tell anybody.

Mac: Mercedes, that secretary from HR, was in the cafeteria. You know her, Victor. She's the office gossip. She knows everything and talks to everyone in the office. I was getting a cup of coffee, and she was talking to her friends. She has a loud voice, and I overheard her.

Victor: I didn't get the job.

Mac: What? Are you kidding? Why not? You're one of the best employees in this department. Everybody here knows that Anthony is going to retire soon. I think everybody expects you to be the new supervisor. You have the most experience and everyone likes you.

Victor: Thanks, Mac. I appreciate your support, but there's nothing I can do about it.

Mac: What do you mean? Did they hire somebody's relative? A cousin? A nephew?

Victor: I don't think anyone has the job yet. I didn't get the job because the company requires a high school diploma for the job. I don't have a high school diploma.

You're Late!

Get Ready to Read

A Discuss with a partner.

1. What is Victor going to say to his wife, Marisa, about the promotion?
2. What is Marisa going to answer?
3. What is Victor going to do right now?

B Match the words with the definitions.

_e_ 1. advise

_____ 2. wonder

_____ 3. apologize

_____ 4. an excuse

_____ 5. reassure

_____ 6. (to be) gone

_____ 7. freeze (at work)

a. not there; no more

b. say you're sorry

c. a reason; usually not a good reason

d. no more new employees or promotions

e. give someone suggestions or counseling

f. make someone feel better

g. think about

In the last episode...

After Victor leaves Mr. Stevenson's office, he goes back to his job in the mailroom. His friend and co-worker, Mac, knows about the interview and is surprised that Victor didn't get the promotion. Victor tells Mac why he didn't get the job. Mac is surprised to hear that Victor doesn't have a diploma, and he encourages Victor to try to get one. Victor is very worried about his family's reaction to the bad news about the promotion. When he arrives home, he sees that there are a lot of cars parked in front of his house and on his street.

🎧 It's about 6:30 when Victor gets home. He walks slowly to the house because he's thinking about the interview. His friend and co-worker, Mac, **advised** him to get his high school diploma or a GED, but Victor isn't sure what to do. He doesn't want to attend school with teenagers, but he thinks that he wants a regular diploma and not a GED. Then he thinks about his family. He knows that Marisa will be disappointed about the promotion. He has two children, a 17-year-old daughter in high school and an 11-year-old son in middle school. "Do the kids know about the promotion, too?" Victor **wonders**.

Victor hears music coming from his house. He sees that all the lights are on, and he sees his father-in-law's car in front of the house. His youngest sister's car is in the driveway. Victor decides to look into the kitchen. He quietly walks to the side of the house and up the steps to the kitchen door. "What is going on?" he thinks.

"Oh, no!" Victor says to himself. "Marisa is having a party. I know it's a party for me. What am I going to tell everyone?" Victor starts to walk back down the steps very slowly and quietly. His dog, Fred, suddenly starts to **bark**.* The door begins to open, so Victor runs around to the back of the house. He sees another sister's motorcycle in the backyard. Victor decides to leave. "I'm getting out of here!" he thinks. Fred stops barking, and Victor goes back to his car. No one sees him. He gets into his car and drives away.

Victor drives around the neighborhood. "Marisa is going to wonder where I am. I have one message from her on the phone. Maybe if I stay away for a couple of hours, everyone will go home. Then I can explain everything."

Two hours later at about 8:30, Victor's wife, Marisa, is saying good-bye to her in-laws and friends. Two of Victor's sisters, Ana and Luisa, are at the back door.

*bark = the noise a dog makes

Marisa **apologizes** to her sisters-in-law, "I'm sorry Victor isn't here. I don't know where he is, and he isn't answering his cell phone. I'm getting worried. Maybe I should call the police."

"The police? Wait a little longer. It's only 8:30, Marisa," says Ana. "I'm sure he has a good **excuse**. Maybe he's working overtime. It's not unusual for him to work late, is it?"

"No, but he always calls when he's going to be late," says Marisa.

Luisa tries to **reassure** Marisa. "Don't worry," she says, "I'm sure my big brother is OK. We'll celebrate another time. Are you sure that we can't help you clean up?"

"Thanks, Lu," says Marisa. "Your mom and dad are going to help." She gives her sisters-in-law big hugs. "It won't take long to clean up. I'll call you when he gets home."

Luisa opens the door. Her boyfriend is on his motorcycle and ready to go. "Call me, Marisa. Gene is waiting for me. Bye."

"I have to go, too. The babysitter will be glad to go home early. I'm sure Victor is fine, Marisa," says Ana.

After everyone is gone, Marisa looks around the kitchen. There are plates of food all over the kitchen table. There are a few empty bottles on the kitchen counter. In the dining room, there are decorations hanging from the ceiling. Their son, Jordan, made a sign. It says, "Congratulations, Dad!" Marisa says to herself, "Where are you, Victor?"

Victor's father, Ricardo, comes into the kitchen carrying a trash bag. "I collected all of the trash from the living room. I'm going to put this in the garbage can. I'll take Fred for a walk. Come on, Fred." Ricardo takes Fred outside.

Iris, Victor's mother, comes into the kitchen. "So, Victor isn't home yet?" she asks.

"No," says Marisa. "He's not here, and he's not answering his cell phone. This is very unusual for him."

"Maybe he's getting a surprise for you and the kids," says Iris. "I'm sure he'll be home soon. Let's clean up the kitchen."

* * * *

About an hour later, Fred starts barking again. Victor opens the door and walks into the kitchen. He pets Fred and gives him a dog treat. Fred goes to his blanket and lies down. Victor looks around the kitchen. Everything is clean. It's quiet. There is no sign of a party. Victor walks into the dining room, and all the decorations **are gone** except the sign that Jordan made. It is on the dining room table. When Victor sees the sign, he feels bad. He calls, "Marisa, honey. Are you down here?"

In the living room, Marisa is asleep on the sofa, and the TV is on. Victor sits down next to her and kisses her on the cheek. Marisa opens her eyes and looks at Victor.

"Where were you?" Marisa says. She looks sleepy but angry.

"I had to work late. I'm sorry that I didn't call."

"Didn't call?" Marisa is **wide awake*** now. "I was worried! I was going to call the police, but your sisters told me to wait a little longer. I had a party for you tonight. Did you know that? Your sisters were here, my father and your parents were here, and the kids decorated the dining room. A few of our neighbors were here, too. Everyone was very polite, but I know they were very disappointed! And I took half a day off from work to come home early to put this party together." Marisa is standing now, with her hands on her hips. She looks very angry.

Victor looks away and lies to his wife, "I'm really sorry. I didn't know about the party."

Suddenly Marisa remembers why she wanted to have a party. "What about the promotion? What happened?"

"I didn't get it."

"What? What do you mean? I thought . . . "

*__wide awake__ = completely awake; not sleepy

"I didn't get it," says Victor. "The company is laying off employees, so they're not going to give out any promotions now."

"But you had an interview."

"It wasn't really an interview. They told me that there was a **freeze** on all promotions."

"A freeze? I don't understand. Why didn't they cancel your interview?"

Victor begins to get angry, "I don't know, Marisa! Maybe because I'm a good employee. Who knows? All I know is that I didn't get the promotion! I still have a job. Can we stop talking about it?"

Marisa apologizes, "I'm sorry, sweetie. I didn't know. The party wasn't a good idea."

Their children, Alexandra and Jordan, come down the stairs. They look worried. They heard their father's voice.

"Is anything wrong?" asks Jordan.

Reading Comprehension

A Circle *True* or *False.*

1. Victor wants to go into his house.		True	False
2. Victor parked his car in the driveway.		True	False
3. Marisa is worried about Victor.		True	False
4. Ana and Luisa are worried about their brother.		True	False
5. Victor never works overtime.		True	False
6. Marisa has a good relationship with her sisters-in-law.		True	False
7. Ana's children came to the party.		True	False
8. Marisa's mother-in-law is helping her clean up.		True	False

B Circle the correct answer.

1. Victor came home _____ late.
   a. an hour
   b. two hours
   c. three hours
   d. more than three hours

2. Who came to the party?
   a. Victor's family and in-laws
   b. Neighbors
   c. Victor's co-workers
   d. both a and b

3. Marisa is angry because _____.
   a. Victor didn't get the promotion
   b. Victor's family didn't help her clean up
   c. she spent a lot of time preparing for the party
   d. Victor didn't help with the party

4. According to Victor, which sentence is <u>not</u> true?
   a. TabLet has a freeze on all promotions.
   b. TabLet is laying off employees.
   c. He is going to be laid off.
   d. Marisa was worried about her husband.

C Complete the sentences.

1. What did the family do to prepare for the party?

   Jordan _____.

   Marisa _____.

   They invited _____.

2. Victor gave Marisa a reason why he didn't get the promotion. What was it?

   _____.

Work with the Words

(A) Circle the correct answer.

1. The college counselor **advised** me about _____.
   a. my vacation plans   c. my car trouble
   b. my courses   d. the morning traffic

2. It is cloudy today. I **wonder** if _____.
   a. it's cloudy   c. it's sunny
   b. it rained yesterday   d. it's going to rain today

3. My _____ **barks** when a delivery man comes to our house.
   a. doorbell   c. bird
   b. husband   d. dog

4. Bob's sister **apologized** because she _____.
   a. forgot to pick him up on time
   b. picked him up early
   c. remembered his birthday
   d. gave him a present

5. Which is a good **excuse** for not doing homework?
   a. I didn't have time.
   b. I had to work overtime, so I didn't have time.
   c. I had to go to a party.
   d. My favorite TV program was on.

6. After I failed the driving test, my parents **reassured** me that
   _____.
   a. the car was not working   c. I could take it again
   b. they couldn't help me   d. it was my last chance

7. All of the tickets to the final game were **gone** when I got to the
   ticket window because _____.
   a. no one wanted to buy them   c. I arrived early
   b. I had enough money   d. I was last in line

8. There was a **freeze** on hiring new employees because _____.

   a. there were many poor employees   **c.** sales were good

   b. sales were bad   **d.** the weather was cold

9. I was **wide awake** after I drank _____.

   a. some milk   **c.** some lemonade

   b. some water   **d.** some coffee

B **Complete the sentences with the correct words and phrases. You will not use all the words.**

advised	excuse	reassured
apologize	freeze	wide awake
bark	gone	wonder

1. Beverly didn't want to date Frank again, so she gave him an _____.

2. The police officer _____ the driver to drive more slowly.

3. The mother _____ her child that she would always be there.

4. The mother had to get up early because her baby was _____ at 5:00 A.M.

5. There is a _____ on hiring new employees because business is very poor right now.

6. I _____ for arriving late again. I'm really sorry.

7. My dog is not a good watchdog. He doesn't _____.

C Match the word with the sentence.

—— **1.** advise   **a.** I'm sorry that I broke your cup.

—— **2.** excuse   **b.** Don't worry. Everything will be fine.

—— **3.** apologize   **c.** I left my homework at home.

—— **4.** reassure   **d.** I think you should go back to school.

Lifeskill Practice

■ It's useful to be able to talk about problems at work.

A Complete the conversations. Use the words from the box.

freeze on promotions	hiring freeze	lay off

1. **A:** What's wrong?

   B: I applied for a promotion, but there's a _____.

   A: Why?

   B: Business is slow.

2. **A:** What's wrong?

   B: The company is going to _____ 50 people in my department.

   A: Why?

   B: Sales are poor.

3. **A:** What's wrong?

   B: I need a better job, but many companies have a

   _____.

   A: Really? Why?

   B: The economy is slow right now. Nobody wants to hire anyone new.

B Practice the conversations in Exercise A with a partner.

C Write a new conversation with the words in Exercise A. Use your imagination.

A: What's wrong?

B: _____.

A: Really? Why?

B: _____

Dialogue Practice

Practice the dialogue with a classmate.

Marisa: What about the promotion? What happened?

Victor: I didn't get it.

Marisa: What? What do you mean? I thought . . .

Victor: I didn't get it. The company is laying off employees, so they're not going to give out any promotions now.

Marisa: But you had an interview.

Victor: It wasn't really an interview. They told me that there was a freeze on all promotions.

Marisa: A freeze? I don't understand. Why didn't they cancel your interview?

Victor: I don't know, Marisa! Maybe because I'm a good employee. Who knows? All I know is that I didn't get the promotion! I still have a job! Can we stop talking about it?

Marisa: I'm sorry, sweetie. I didn't know. The party wasn't a good idea.

An Excuse

34

Get Ready to Read

A Discuss with a partner.

1. Why does Victor look upset?
2. What is he going to do?
3. What is Marisa going to say to the children?

B Match the words and expressions with the definitions.

__f__ 1. senior (in school)

_____ 2. anymore

_____ 3. unfortunately

_____ 4. honor roll

_____ 5. Advanced Placement

_____ 6. scholarship

_____ 7. reference

a. gift of money for school

b. opposite of fortunately; unluckily

c. a letter or phone call from an employer

d. no longer; no more time

e. a list of students with good grades

f. a student in the last year of high school or college

g. difficult classes that can give high school students college credit

In the last episode...

Victor's wife, Marisa, planned a party to celebrate Victor's promotion. Victor didn't want a party, so he stayed away from home until it was over. He didn't call, and when he came home, Marisa was angry that he didn't call and embarrassed about the party. Victor told Marisa that there was a hiring freeze, and that's why he didn't get the promotion. Marisa thought that it was strange and asked Victor to explain more about it. Victor began to get angry. At that moment, his children, Jordan and Alexandra, came downstairs to see what was going on.

🎧 Victor's children, Alexandra and Jordan, are coming down the stairs. Alexandra is 17 years old and a senior in high school. Jordan is 11 and in middle school. At first, they smile when they see their father, because they're expecting to hear good news about the promotion. Then they are concerned because both of their parents look upset. Victor is angry because Marisa is asking too many questions.

"Is anything wrong?" asks Jordan.

"Nothing's wrong," answers Victor. "I'm just tired. I'll see you in the morning."

"But Dad, what about the . . . ?" asks Jordan, but Victor doesn't answer. He goes upstairs.

"What's wrong with Dad?" asks Alexandra. "Didn't he get the promotion?"

"No, he didn't, Alex," says Marisa, "and don't talk about it **anymore**. Your father is pretty disappointed."

The next morning, everyone is in the kitchen getting ready for work or school. Jordan is outside walking Fred. Alexandra is **pouring** cereal and milk into bowls for herself and Jordan, and Victor is making coffee. It's quiet except for the sound of the radio playing the morning news.

Jordan comes back into the kitchen with Fred. "Go to your bed, Fred," says Jordan. Fred goes to his dog bed in the corner and lies down. Jordan washes his hands and sits down for breakfast. Everyone is looking at Victor because he's not talking. Victor is a **morning person**,* so he is usually in a good mood and is very talkative in the morning.

*morning person = a person who has a lot of energy in the morning

Victor looks at his family. "I want to apologize. I'm sorry about last night, everybody. I know you wanted to congratulate me and have a party with our friends and family. You **went to a lot of trouble*** to celebrate my promotion. **Unfortunately**, I didn't get it."

Alexandra gets up and hugs her father. "Dad, it's OK. Don't worry about it."

"Alex, you're a **senior** in high school. We're going to need money for college next year."

Marisa says, "Listen Victor. You know that Alex is an excellent student. She received almost all As and one B plus last period, so she's on the **honor roll** again, and she's taking three **Advanced Placement** classes. She's taking two honors courses, too. It's a very, very difficult schedule. If Alex gets college credit for a few of those AP courses, we can save money next year because she won't have to take those classes in college. And, of course, she's going to apply for **scholarships**. Remember, we're already getting letters from colleges that have good soccer teams. She's the captain of the girls' soccer team this year, and she was on the All State soccer team for the third time. Maybe she'll get a soccer scholarship or an academic scholarship. I'm sure that we're going to get some financial help." She puts her hand on Victor's shoulder.

Victor grabs Marisa's hand and kisses it. He says, "I know we're going to be OK, but college **tuition**** is getting higher every year. It's going to be even more expensive when it's time for Jordan to go to school."

"Don't worry, Dad. I'm not going to go to college. I'm going to be a professional baseball player."

"A baseball player?" says Victor. "If you continue playing like you played at that game last week, you're not going to be on the team. I want you to study harder, Jordan. I don't want to see any more Cs on your report card."

"OK, Dad," says Jordan.

"Anyway, Marisa," says Victor, "We need to be prepared. I know that you're all disappointed that I didn't get the promotion. I'm going to apply again when things are better at the company."

"Good idea, Dad," says Jordan, "Maybe I can write a **reference** for you." He smiles.

***went to a lot of trouble** = did a lot in order to complete a job or favor

****tuition** = costs for colleges or private or religious schools

Victor puts his hand on Jordan's head and rubs his very short hair. "Thanks, Jordan. I'm sure your reference will help me get a promotion—as a baseball coach." Everyone laughs.

"Oh, I forgot. Yesterday, the manager of Human Resources told me that all employees will have to work more overtime for a while. There's a big project, and everyone will have to help. I think the company is going to transfer me to a different department for a while. There are going to be some layoffs at the company, so everyone is going to have to work longer hours."

"Layoffs? More overtime?" asks Marisa. "But you already work on Saturday mornings. You work in the mailroom. Why do they need you to work overtime?"

Victor looks angry. "I told you that there are going to be some layoffs. I know that I only work in the mailroom, and that you are an important office manager, but my job is important, too. And, tonight, I'm going to be home late."

"Oh, Victor, I didn't mean . . . "

Victor stands up, gets his jacket, and walks out, slamming the door.

"Nice work, Mom," says Alexandra. "Dad was beginning to feel better. Now he feels worse." She gets up and puts her dishes in the dishwasher.

"You're right. I'll apologize later. Maybe I'll plan something special for dinner tonight."

Everyone gets ready to leave.

Reading Comprehension

A Circle *True* or *False*.

1. Marisa is a nurse.	True	False
2. Victor's son and daughter are in college.	True	False
3. Everyone helps in the morning.	True	False
4. Victor is usually quiet in the morning.	True	False
5. Alex is upset about her father's promotion.	True	False
6. Alex is an excellent student and athlete.	True	False
7. Alex is working full-time to get money for college.	True	False
8. Alex is getting good grades because she is taking easy classes.	True	False

B Circle the correct answer.

1. When is Victor going to apply for another promotion?
   a. tomorrow   **c.** never
   b. after he gets his diploma   **d.** after Alex is in college

2. Jordan is _____ about his father's future at the company.
   a. nervous   **c.** not happy
   b. upset   **d.** not worried

3. Jordan plays _____.
   a. baseball   **c.** soccer
   b. basketball   **d.** volleyball

4. How does Marisa feel about Victor's new work schedule?
   a. She likes it.
   b. She doesn't care.
   c. She is excited but nervous.
   d. She's angry and surprised.

C Answer the questions.

1. Describe Alexandra (Alex).

_____

_____

2. Describe Jordan.

_____

_____

3. How are Victor and Marisa planning to pay for Alex's college tuition?

_____

_____

4. Why does Victor say he has to work extra overtime?

_____

_____

Work with the Words

A Circle the correct answer.

1. *I am not living in Brazil anymore* means _____.
   a. I don't live in Brazil now.
   b. I want to live in Brazil.
   c. I don't want to live in Brazil.
   d. I don't speak to my family every day.

2. Alexandra is **pouring** cereal and milk into bowls. What else can you pour?
   a. paper
   b. water
   c. meat
   d. rice

3. I'm a **morning person**, so I like to _____.
   a. sleep late
   b. get up early and work
   c. stay in bed
   d. work late in the evening

4. My family **went to a lot of trouble** to help our cousin. This means
_____.

   a. they did a lot   **c.** they made one phone call
   b. they did nothing   **d.** they were angry

5. I wanted to go to the park. **Unfortunately,** _____.

   a. it was a beautiful day   **c.** it was cool and rainy
   b. it was sunny and warm   **d.** it was the best day of the
                                           summer

6. Donny is on the **honor roll** because he _____.

   a. failed all of his courses   **c.** helps the teacher
   b. is a good student   **d.** is a good soccer player

7. _____ will receive a **scholarship**.

   a. An average basketball player with poor grades
   b. A good basketball player with average grades
   c. A lazy student with poor grades
   d. A very good student with excellent grades

8. My _____ wrote a **reference** when I wanted a promotion.

   a. best friend   **c.** landlord
   b. grandmother   **d.** boss

B Complete the conversations with the correct words and phrases.
You will not use all the words.

anymore	go to a lot of trouble	morning person	pour

1. **A:** I'll fix you some breakfast.

   B: Don't _____.

   A: It's not a problem. I'll make some pancakes.

   B: I'm not really hungry. I'm not a _____. Could you

   just _____ some coffee for me?

references	scholarship	senior	unfortunately

2. **A:** What grade are you in?

   B: I'm a _____.

   A: How can I help you?

   B: I would like to apply for a _____.

   A: OK. First, I need three _____ from teachers.

Lifeskill Practice

Talking about school

Alex is a **senior** in high school. She is in twelfth grade. A **junior** is in eleventh grade; a **sophomore** is in tenth grade; and a **freshman** is in ninth grade. She's on the honor roll because her grades are very good, and she's taking several Advanced Placement (AP) classes. She also plays **soccer**, and she's hoping to get a scholarship to help with college **tuition**.

Pairs. Tell your partner about a high school student you know. You can start like this:

My son is a **sophomore** in high school. Last year he was a **freshman**, and his grades weren't good. This year he's doing better, and he hopes to be on the **honor roll** soon. He really likes sports; he plays soccer, basketball, and baseball. He thinks he's going to get an athletic **scholarship**, but I'm hoping his grades will improve, too.

Dialogue Practice

Practice the conversation with three classmates.

Victor: I want to apologize. I'm sorry about last night, everybody. I know you wanted to congratulate me and have a party with our friends and family. You went to a lot of trouble to celebrate my promotion. Unfortunately, I didn't get it.

Alexandra: Dad, it's OK. Don't worry about it.

Victor: Alex, you're a senior in high school. We're going to need money for college next year.

Marisa: Listen, Victor. You know that Alex is an excellent student. She received almost all As and one B plus last period, so she's on the honor roll again, and she's taking three Advanced Placement classes. She's taking two honors courses, too. It's a very, very difficult schedule. If Alex gets college credit for a few of those AP courses, we can save money next year because she won't have to take those classes in college. And, of course, she's going to apply for scholarships. Remember, we're already getting letters from colleges that have good soccer teams. She's the captain of the girls' soccer team this year, and she was on the All State soccer team for the third time. Maybe she'll get a soccer scholarship or an academic scholarship. I'm sure that we're going to get some financial help.

Victor: I know we're going to be OK, but college tuition is getting higher every year. It's going to be even more expensive when it's time for Jordan to go to college.

Jordan: Don't worry, Dad. I'm not going to go to college. I'm going to be a professional baseball player.

Victor: A baseball player? If you continue playing like you played at that game last week, you're not going to be on the team. I want you to study harder, Jordan. I don't want to see any more Cs on your report card.

The Plan

Get Ready to Read

A Discuss with a partner.

1. Why is Victor angry?
2. Do you think he's right to be angry?
3. What should Marisa do?

B Match the words and expressions with the definitions.

___f___ 1. supportive   **a.** do well; succeed

_____ 2. in a bad mood   **b.** say you will do something

_____ 3. whole   **c.** feel happy because you or someone else did something good

_____ 4. pass (a test)

_____ 5. find out   **d.** all; entire

_____ 6. proud   **e.** angry; upset

_____ 7. promise   **f.** helps or encourages others

    g. learn new information

In the last episode...

Victor tells Marisa about his interview, and now his children, Alexandra and Jordan, know about it, too. The next morning at breakfast, Victor apologizes for not coming to the party and explains that he is worried about how they are going to pay for Alexandra's college tuition next year. Marisa reminds Victor that Alexandra is a good student, so she will probably receive scholarships. Everyone is very supportive and encourages Victor to try again for the promotion later, but Marisa gets upset when Victor tells her that he has to work overtime on a special project. She wonders why a mailroom employee needs to work so much overtime. Victor gets angry and leaves for work.

🎧 Victor is in his car on the way to work. He's angry, so he's talking to himself. "I can't believe it! Marisa doesn't respect my job. How could she say that? I have responsibilities, too. I'll show her. After I get my diploma, I'll have a better job. I'll make more money, and I'll pay for Alex's tuition next year. Maybe we'll buy a new car. Maybe we'll buy a bigger house."

Victor is usually a friendly, talkative person. All of his co-workers like him, and he gets along well with everyone, but today Victor is **in a bad mood**. He isn't talking to anyone, and he looks angry.

Finally, Mac says, "Victor, can you come over here for a minute?"

"What do you want?" Victor says. He's frowning and looks angry.

"Hey, Victor. What's wrong with you? You're in a bad mood today. Did something happen at home?"

"I'm sorry, Mac. When I got home last night, there was a surprise party. Marisa told my **whole** family about the promotion."

Mac puts his hand on Victor's shoulder. "I'm sorry, Victor. What did everyone say when you told them that you didn't get the promotion?"

"Nothing. I didn't go to the party. I waited until everyone was gone."

"What? Are you kidding me? **I bet*** Marisa was furious!"

"She was. When I got home, she was angry, but then I told her that I didn't get the promotion. But I didn't tell her the real reason why I didn't get the promotion."

"Why not? Marisa will understand."

"No, she won't." Victor looks down at the floor.

"Victor," asks Mac, "does Marisa know that you don't have a high school diploma?"

Victor says nothing.

"She doesn't know?!" asks Mac.

Victor answers, "No, she doesn't know. Of course, my sisters and my parents know, but I never told Marisa."

"Why not, Victor? She's your wife. You always say that she is very **supportive**. You always tell me that she listens to all of your problems about work."

"I know, but I don't think she will understand now, especially after all of these years. And my kids won't understand either. I always tell them that

*****I bet** = I think; I guess

education is very important for their future. How can I tell them that their father didn't finish high school?"

"But Victor, you're going to go back to school. They're going to **find out** anyway."

"I know. I'll tell them after I have my diploma. I just have to find a good school to attend."

"Listen, Victor. I made some calls and searched on the Internet. You're **in luck**.* There's a new course starting at the high school. It's an intensive course called Second Chance, for adults who dropped out of high school. It meets five nights a week for eight weeks. At the end, you'll take some tests. If you **pass**, you'll get a diploma. Look. Here's the information." Mac hands Victor some papers.

Victor looks at the information and says, "Mac, thanks a lot. This sounds like a great course. I'll go to the school tonight."

"But what are you going to tell Marisa? Isn't she going to wonder why you're working late every night?"

"Yeah, but I told her that I'm going to be working on a special project and will have to work overtime. I knew that I would have to take some kind of course at night. I wanted to keep it a secret."

"But for eight weeks?" asks Mac.

"I'll only have to keep it a secret for two months. Then, they'll be **proud** of me."

Mac looks at Victor. "Victor, I'm sure your family is proud of you now. You have a good job. You support your family. You're a good father."

Victor says quietly, "I'm not going to tell them. Please don't say anything. I'm more worried about Alex. I . . . "

A supervisor sees that Mac and Victor are having a long conversation. "Mac, Victor! We have to deliver these packages before lunchtime."

Mac and Victor get back to work. They will talk again at lunch.

Later, Victor and Mac are having lunch in the cafeteria. Mac **promises** not to say anything about Victor's secret.

"You said that you were worried about Alex. Are you afraid that she is going to see you at school?" Mac asks.

Victor says, "I'm a little worried, but the information that you gave me says that my classes will begin at 5:30. Alex finishes school at three o'clock, and soccer practice keeps her pretty busy after that. Also, the soccer field is about ten minutes from the school."

*in luck = You're lucky.

"I don't know Victor," says Mac. "Someone's going to see you at the high school. One of her friends might see you.

"Don't worry about it. Everything will be fine. I'll be careful."

*   *   *   *

That evening at 7:30, Marisa is in the kitchen. Alexandra and Jordan are finishing their dinner. Marisa is very quiet, and the children don't know what to say. Victor is not home.

"Mom, where's Dad?" asks Jordan.

"He's working overtime, Jordan. Remember? He told us this morning," says Marisa. She's preparing a plate of dinner for Victor to have later.

"But it's 7:30. He's usually home by now. I need help with my homework," says Jordan.

Marisa puts the plate in the refrigerator and answers, "I'll help you after I clean up."

"But you don't do it the same way. I'll wait for Dad."

Marisa slams the dishes in the sink. "Go upstairs, Jordan. Alex, you, too. Go upstairs with your brother. I'm sure you have homework, too."

"Mom, I'll clean up," says Alex.

"That's OK, Alex. You have homework. I'll clean up tonight. You can help tomorrow."

"Are you sure?" asks Alex.

"I'm sure. Go do your homework."

"OK, Mom." Alex kisses her mother on the cheek. "Everything will be fine, Mom."

Reading Comprehension

A Circle *True* or *False*.

1.	Victor feels good today.	**True**	**False**
2.	Victor is usually talkative at work.	**True**	**False**
3.	Mac was at the party at Victor's house.	**True**	**False**
4.	Victor told Marisa the truth about the promotion.	**True**	**False**
5.	Victor's sisters know that he doesn't have a diploma.	**True**	**False**
6.	Mac gave Victor information about a special course.	**True**	**False**
7.	Victor plans to start the special course next week.	**True**	**False**
8.	Victor is going to join Alexandra's high school classes.	**True**	**False**

B Circle the correct answer.

1. Who knows that Victor doesn't have a diploma?
   a. everyone
   b. no one
   c. his sisters
   d. Marisa

2. How often does the special program meet?
   a. five nights a week
   b. six nights a week
   c. every weekend
   d. every morning

3. What did Victor tell Marisa?
   a. He is going to take a special class.
   b. He is going to work overtime.
   c. He is going to change jobs.
   d. He is going to get a promotion.

4. Why does Victor have to be careful when he goes to the high school?
   a. His wife might see him there.
   b. His son might see him there.
   c. His daughter or her friends might see him there.
   d. Mac might see him there.

C Who said it? Read each sentence. Circle the name of the correct character.

1. You're in a bad mood.	Mac	Victor
2. I always say that education is important for their future.	Mac	Victor
3. They'll be proud of me.	Mac	Victor
4. Marisa will be supportive.	Mac	Victor
5. I'm sorry.	Mac	Victor
6. You have a good job.	Mac	Victor

Work with the Words

A Circle the correct answer.

1. After the boys lost the game, their parents were very **supportive.** They _____.
   a. told them to practice for four more hours
   b. were angry
   c. told them not to worry about it and to think about the next game
   d. were happy that they lost

2. Jessica is **in a bad mood**. She is usually talkative and friendly, but this morning, she _____.

   a. looks angry and is not talking to anyone

   b. is more talkative and very friendly

   c. is talking to everyone

   d. is friendlier than usual

3. Mac thinks that Victor's daughter is going to **find out** about his classes. She is _____.

   a. going to hear a secret

   b. going to write some information

   c. going to go somewhere

   d. going to tell a secret

4. Mac **promises** not to say anything. Mac won't _____.

   a. tell Victor's family   **c.** tell anyone

   b. tell Mercedes   **d.** tell Anthony

5. Don's family is **proud** of him because he _____.

   a. was fired from his job   **c.** graduated from college

   b. dropped out of high school   **d.** failed his courses

6. My best friend is very **supportive**. She _____.

   a. listens and helps me with my problems

   b. doesn't like to listen to my problems

   c. listens but doesn't help me

   d. never helps me

7. My **whole** class is here today. Who is here?

   a. everyone except three students

   b. all of the students

   c. all of the students except one

   d. none of the students

8. That was a really easy test. The whole class _____.

   a. did really well   **c.** apologized

   b. found out   **d.** went to a lot of trouble

B Complete the paragraphs with the correct words and phrases. You will not use all the words.

find out	in a bad mood	promises	supportive
I bet	in luck	proud	whole

1. Lucia is lucky that her boss is very _____. Lucia is sometimes late to work because of her children. She always _____ to come on time, but it takes a long time to get the children ready for school.

2. Lucia is _____ of her oldest son. Mark is a very good student, and he helps her with the younger children. The _____ family thinks he is a wonderful boy.

3. Lucia needs to _____ about preschool programs. Her daughter is old enough to stay in school all day now. Her daughter is excited about going to preschool, so Lucia doesn't think her daughter will cry on the first day of school.

Lifeskill Practice

We use *'ll* plus a verb to give an offer to help.

Example

Marisa: I*'ll help* you after I clean up.

Alex: I*'ll clean* up.

A Practice the conversations.

1. **A:** I don't know how to get to the new post office.
   B: I'll **give** you directions.

2. **A:** This is a difficult homework assignment.
   B: I'll **help** you.

3. **A:** This box is too heavy.
   B: I'll **carry** it for you.

B Complete the conversations. Use the words from the box.

I'll buy it	I'll do it	I'll give you a ride

1. **A:** My car isn't working. I need to get to the bank.

   B: _____.

2. **A:** I really want that T-shirt.

   B: _____ for you.

3. **A:** I don't have time to pack this box.

   B: _____ for you.

C Pairs. Practice the conversations with a partner.

Dialogue Practice

Practice the conversation with a classmate. Act it out.

Mac: Victor, can you come over here for a minute?

Victor: What do you want?

Mac: Hey, Victor. What's wrong with you? You're in a bad mood today. Did something happen at home?

Victor: I'm sorry, Mac. When I got home last night, there was a surprise party. Marisa told my whole family about the promotion.

Mac: I'm sorry, Victor. What did everyone say when you told them that you didn't get the promotion?

Victor: Nothing. I didn't go to the party. I waited until everyone was gone.

Mac: What? Are you kidding me? I bet Marisa was furious!

Victor: She was. When I got home, she was angry, but then I told her that I didn't get the promotion. But I didn't tell her the real reason why I didn't get the promotion.

Mac: Why not? Marisa will understand.

Victor: No, she won't.

Mac: Victor, does Marisa know that you don't have a high school diploma?

Mac: She doesn't know?!

An Excellent Student

Get Ready to Read

A Discuss with a partner.

A Discuss with a partner.

1. How do you think Victor feels right now?
2. What usually happens on the first day of class?
3. How did you feel on your first day of English class?

B Match the words and expressions with the definitions.

_b_ 1. concerned	**a.**	learn more about a person
____ 2. fail	**b.**	worried
____ 3. subjects	**c.**	teach someone, usually one-on-one
____ 4. get to know	**d.**	get better
____ 5. improve	**e.**	do badly; not pass an exam or course
____ 6. miss (class)	**f.**	topics of study
____ 7. tutor	**g.**	not go

In the last episode...

Victor is upset when he gets to work the next morning. He tells Mac about the surprise party. Victor also tells Mac that his wife and children don't know that he doesn't have a diploma. Mac tells Victor that he found information about a special program, Second Chance, for adults who want to get their diplomas. The program starts tonight!

🎧 Victor is walking into the high school. He changed his shirt at work so that none of the students will know where he works. He wants to keep this class a secret. He feels very nervous but also excited.

"Why am I so nervous?" Victor thinks to himself. "I came here last week for a meeting with Alex's teachers."

When Victor finds the room, he is a little **concerned** because it's very large.

"I was hoping for a small class," he thinks.

The room is like a small auditorium. A lot of people are already there. He sits at a desk and waits for the teacher. He starts filling out a form that's on the desk.

A few minutes later, a woman walks into the room and says, "Good evening everyone. I'm Mrs. Williams. Welcome to the Second Chance Program. Tonight all of you will take a **placement test**.* We will be dividing you into classes according to the forms on your desks and your test results. You have two hours for the test. Classes will start on Monday. We will send you a letter and an e-mail with your teacher's name, the room number, and some other important information. Any questions?"

One student asks, "I didn't know that we had to take a test tonight. I didn't study." Victor is thinking the same thing.

"Don't worry," says Mrs. Williams. "This is just a placement test. You can't **fail** it. We want you to be in a class with people with similar experience. Any other questions?"

The room is quiet. Everyone is nervous.

"OK. Let's begin. Please put all of your papers and notebooks under your chairs. Please turn off all cell phones."

*__placement test__ = an exam that students take before a course begins

Victor immediately turns off his cell phone. Another teacher hands him a test. When Mrs. Williams tells them to begin, he opens the test and starts to read.

* * * * *

On Monday night, Victor is ready for his first night of class in the Second Chance Program. The placement exam was a little difficult. Victor was very nervous because it was his first test in many years. He was a good student in high school, but that was a long time ago! The test had six **subjects**: mathematics, social studies, reading and writing, history, and science. Victor was surprised that he felt good after the test was over.

It's 5:20 P.M. when Victor arrives in the classroom. There are about ten other students in the room. Some of them look almost as young as Alex! Before Victor arrived, he thought, "I'm crazy! I will be the oldest student in the class!" but he sees that there are also some students who look about his age or even older, so he feels more relaxed.

A few minutes later, a woman enters the classroom. The woman writes her name, Jean Rogers, on the board. She greets the class, and then she asks everyone to make introductions. "Good evening. My name is Jean Rogers. You can call me Jean. I'll be your instructor for the next eight weeks. Let's **get to know** each other. Please introduce yourselves and tell us why you wanted to join this class."

One by one, the students explain why they are in the class. They came for many different reasons. Some got married very young and didn't finish high school. Some weren't interested in school when they were teenagers. Finally, it's Victor's turn. The teacher asks, "And what's your name?"

Victor doesn't want to talk too much about his personal life. He doesn't want anyone in his family to know what he's doing. Maybe someone in the class knows his wife or his sisters.

"My name is Victor," he says. "I'm in this class because I want and I need a high school diploma. I dropped out of high school when I was sixteen to support my family, but now I'm ready to come back. I want to **improve** my job possibilities and make life better for my family."

Jean smiles and says, "Those are very good reasons, Victor." Then, she says, "Let's get started. We have a lot of work to do."

Three weeks later, Victor is in a great mood. He is enjoying the class very much. Sometimes he arrives a little early to talk to the other students, but he's

always careful not to arrive before five o'clock. Alex studies at the same high school, but she's usually finished by 4:30. He doesn't want her to see him.

At lunchtime at work, Mac asks Victor about the class. "Victor, you're in a great mood. How's the class?"

"Mac," says Victor, "I'm surprised. I'm really enjoying the classes. It's not difficult for me. I'm beginning to remember all the things I learned in high school, but it's not all easy, either. I have a lot of homework."

"When do you do your homework? You can't do it at home," says Mac.

"I know. I stay after class and do the homework with a few of my classmates. Last week I stayed at school until ten o'oclock! Sometimes I can do my homework at home, but I go into my office and close the door. Marisa and the kids are beginning to get upset—I **missed** Jordan's baseball game yesterday, and I forgot about Alex's play at school last week."

"What are you going to do?"

"I don't know. There are five more weeks of the class, and I don't want to miss any classes. It's an intensive program. If I miss one class, I miss a lot. And every week the teacher gives us a practice test to prepare for the final exam. I can't miss a test."

* * * *

Later that evening, Victor is getting ready to leave school after class. He is saying good-bye and walking to his car. One of the students, Vanessa, is waiting on the steps. Vanessa is a very attractive young woman who dropped out of school because she got married young. Now she's 24 and divorced, and she's trying to improve her life.

"Victor, wait a minute," she says.

"What's up, Vanessa?" asks Victor. He puts his key in his car door.

"Victor, you are one of the best students in the class, especially with the math. I'm doing OK in the other subjects, but I'm having trouble with the math. Do you think you could **tutor** me? I really need some extra help."

"Vanessa, I don't have time to tutor you, but I'm working with a few other students after class a few times a week. If you want, you could **join*** us. We like to review our homework together and test each other."

"Thanks a lot," says Vanessa. Then, she hesitates a little. "Victor, would you like to get a cup of coffee with me?"

Reading Comprehension

A Circle *True* or *False*.

1.	Victor was nervous about his first day at school.	True	False
2.	All of the students are Victor's age.	True	False
3.	First, the teacher gives a test.	True	False
4.	All of the students dropped out of high school for the same reason.	True	False
5.	Victor told the truth in his introduction to the class.	True	False
6.	Victor spoke a lot about his family.	True	False
7.	Victor likes the class.	True	False
8.	Victor never arrives for class before 5:30.	True	False

B Circle the correct answer.

1. Which is **not** one of the reasons why the students say they dropped out of high school?

   a. They married young.

   b. They weren't interested in high school.

   c. School was too easy.

   d. They had to work to support their families.

***join** = become member of a group, a team, or a class

2. Why doesn't Victor tell the other students about his family?
   a. Some of his neighbors are in the class.
   b. He doesn't like the other students.
   c. He isn't comfortable with the teacher.
   d. Another student might know his wife or sisters.

3. When does Victor do his homework?
   a. in the evening after the class meets
   b. during the class
   c. during his lunch break
   d. immediately before class begins

4. Why is Victor's family upset with him?
   a. They don't like his class.
   b. Victor is not spending time with his family.
   c. Victor is making more money.
   d. The class is too expensive.

C Answer the questions.

1. Why is Victor in a good mood?

   _____

2. Why doesn't Victor arrive before 5:00 for his class?

   _____

3. Why did Victor forget about Jordan's baseball game?

   _____

4. Why does Vanessa ask Victor for help?

   _____

5. How is Victor going to help Vanessa?

   _____

Work with the Words

A Circle the correct answer.

1. Victor's wife was **concerned** because he _____.
   - **a.** arrived home on time
   - **b.** was very late
   - **c.** enjoyed dinner
   - **d.** helped their children with their homework

2. When do students take **placement exams**?
   - **a.** before a class begins
   - **b.** after a class ends
   - **c.** during their last class
   - **d.** at the end of the first week of class

3. Which one is not a **subject**?
   - **a.** biology
   - **b.** mathematics
   - **c.** English
   - **d.** hiking

4. Let's **get to know** each other means _____.
   - **a.** let's talk about a book
   - **b.** let's talk about our lives
   - **c.** let's talk about the news
   - **d.** let's talk about the class requirements

5. Alan wants to **improve** his job possibilities. He wants to _____.
   - **a.** have a better job
   - **b.** quit his job
   - **c.** have an easier job
   - **d.** work more overtime

6. Toni doesn't want to **miss** her appointment, so she _____.
   - **a.** plans to arrive a little late
   - **b.** isn't going
   - **c.** is going to leave late
   - **d.** is going to go early

7. Vanessa says, "Do you think you could **tutor** me?" Vanessa needs _____.
   - **a.** a different class
   - **b.** some money
   - **c.** extra help
   - **d.** a different teacher

8. If you don't study at all, you will _____ the test.
   - **a.** pass
   - **b.** fail
   - **c.** miss
   - **d.** drop out of

9. She wanted to meet people, so she **joined** a _____.
   - **a.** supermarket
   - **b.** post office
   - **c.** club
   - **d.** school

B Complete the paragraphs. Use the words from the box. You do not need all the words.

concerned	improve	placement exam
fail	join	subjects
get to know	miss	tutor

1. Victor took a long _____ that had many ____subjects____. His teacher, Ms. Rogers, wanted to ___get to know___ the students, so everyone introduced themselves. Victor told everyone that he wanted to ____improve____ his life. The class is important to him, so he doesn't plan to ____miss____ any classes.

2. Vanessa is not doing well in the class, so she was ____concerned____. After class, she asked Victor to ____tutor____ her in math. Victor invited her to ____join____ his study group.

Lifeskill Practice

Small talk is conversation you have with someone when you meet for the first time.

A Read and practice the conversations with a partner. It's OK to use made-up information.

A: Hi, my name's _____. What's yours?

B: My name's _____. Do you live near here?

A: Yes, I do. *OR* No, I don't. How about you?

B: I live in _____ (city).

A: Oh, really? What do you do?

B: I'm a _____ (name of job).

A: How do you like your job?

B: It's _____ (interesting / good / great / boring). How about you? What do you do?

A: I work / study at _____ (name of company or school).

B: What do you do there?

A: I _____ .

B: Really? My _____ (brother / sister / cousin / friend) works there. Do you know _____ (him / her)?

A: What's _____ (his / her) name?

B: _____ (his / her) name is _____ (name).

A: Sorry, I don't know _____ (him / her).

Dialogue Practice

Practice the conversation with a classmate.

Vanessa: Victor, wait a minute.

Victor: What's up, Vanessa?

Vanessa: Victor, you are one of the best students in the class, especially with the math. I'm doing OK in the other subjects, but I'm having trouble with the math. Do you think you could tutor me? I really need some extra help.

Victor: Vanessa, I don't have time to tutor you, but I am working with a few other students after class a few times a week. If you want, you could join us. We like to review our homework together and test each other.

Vanessa: Thanks a lot. Victor, would you like to get a cup of coffee with me?

An Unexpected Invitation

Get Ready to Read

A Discuss with a partner.

1. Who is Vanessa?
2. Why do you think Vanessa invited Victor to go out for coffee?
3. Do you think Victor will have coffee with her?

B Match the words and expressions with the definitions.

_f_ 1. share

_____ 2. jealous

_____ 3. take turns

_____ 4. tough

_____ 5. notes

_____ 6. snack

_____ 7. flattered

a. difficult

b. information that a student writes down during class

c. something to eat between meals

d. first one person, then another person

e. feel good about a compliment

f. use something with another person

g. angry or upset because someone is showing attention to your friend, girlfriend, boyfriend, or spouse, or because someone has something that you want

In the last episode...

Victor started the Second Chance program. He took a placement test before classes began. Now after three weeks in the program, Victor is enjoying school. He's one of the best students in his class, especially in math. Today after class, a beautiful young student named Vanessa asked him to tutor her and invited Victor out for coffee. What's he going to do?

"Victor, would you like to get a cup of coffee with me?" asks Vanessa.

"Uh . . . uh. I don't know, Vanessa," Victor says nervously.

"Come on. Just a cup of coffee, Victor. We can talk about the class, and we can get to know each other better."

Victor is thinking to himself, "Get to know each other better? I'm probably twenty years older than she is. Is she **asking me out**?"*

Victor finally speaks, "Thanks, Vanessa. I'm very **flattered**, but it's late, and . . . I'm married."

"Oh," says Vanessa. She looks disappointed. "You're married? I didn't know. Well, thanks for inviting me to join your study group. See you."

Vanessa goes to her car, but Victor is still standing next to his car. He's starting to smile. "Hmm. How about that? I got an invitation from a beautiful young woman. Marisa is pretty **jealous** of other women. I will be in trouble with Marisa if she finds out that a young girl like that asked me out." Victor laughs and drives home.

* * * *

That week, Victor and his study group are meeting on a Saturday morning. The class is halfway through the program, and they have a midterm exam on Monday and Tuesday. They're all very nervous about it, so they decided to meet today. Victor felt a little anxious about meeting in a public place because he didn't want any of his friends or family to see him. His family thinks that he is at work. Fortunately, the group is meeting in another town today. One of the students, Roberto, has to go to work right after the study session, so they're meeting at a coffee shop near his job.

The study group works well together. The students **take turns** testing each other in the subjects they know best. Victor is in charge of math, Roberto is in charge of science, Vanessa explains all of the reading and writing, and Janet does American history. Janet is a **tough** teacher. She expects everyone to answer all of her questions correctly and to explain their answers. Finally, Lee Ann's specialty is geography. Geography is part of the social studies section. It's Lee Ann's favorite subject. She brings in pictures of mountains, rivers, and cities to help everyone learn. The group divides up the rest of the social studies: economics,

---

*ask someone out = ask someone for a date

politics, and government. They have a lot of subjects to study, but the study group helps everyone.

After a couple hours, Vanessa says, "Why don't we take a break?"

"Good idea, Vanessa," says Janet. "This is a good place to stop. I have to go pick up my grandson. I promised to take him to the movies. Can I get your **notes** on Monday?"

"Sure, Janet," says Vanessa.

Then Roberto looks at his watch and says, "It's after twelve. Sorry, but I have to go, too. I have to be at work in twenty minutes, and I need to change into my uniform first. See you Monday."

"See you. Have a good weekend," says Victor.

Lee Ann, Vanessa, and Victor are the only ones left at the table. "Well," says Victor, "why don't we take a short break, and then go over Lee Ann's practice questions?"

"Good idea," says Lee Ann. "I prepared some good questions for you." Lee Ann gets up from the table. "Does anyone want anything? I need a **snack** and another cup of coffee."

Victor says, "No thanks, Lee Ann."

Vanessa doesn't want anything either. "Thanks, Lee Ann. I have some water."

Lee Ann goes to the counter to get her coffee. Victor starts looking for his geography notes.

Vanessa looks at Victor and says, "Victor?"

Victor answers, "Yeah?"

Vanessa looks down at her papers and says, "Thank you for inviting me to join the study group, Victor."

Victor answers, "Not at all, Vanessa."

"I really needed help with the math, but you're all helping me with the other subjects, too. I feel much more confident now. I think I can pass the exam."

Victor smiles and says, "Me, too. I really like studying in a group. Everyone has something different to add to the group."

Then Vanessa asks, "This was your idea, wasn't it?"

"Well, actually," Victor says, "Roberto and I both thought it was a good idea. Then we talked to Lee Ann and Janet."

"It was a great idea. By the way, I'm sorry about asking you out. I didn't know you were married. I guess you thought I was crazy." Vanessa puts her hand on Victor's hand.

"Well, yeah, a little bit," says Victor, "but that's OK, Vanessa. I was flattered. It's not every day that a young woman like you asks a middle-aged man like me out for coffee." They both laugh.

"VICTOR! WHAT ARE YOU DOING?"

It's Iris, Victor's mother! She's standing next to Vanessa, who moves her hand away immediately. Iris is looking back and forth between Victor and Vanessa. Victor looks very embarrassed.

"Mom! Uh . . . Hi! What are you doing here?" Victor asks nervously.

"What am I doing here? I am having lunch with some friends. What are you doing here with this . . . this woman?"

Victor looks at Vanessa. "Mom, this is . . . " Before he can finish, Lee Ann comes back to the table.

Lee Ann has a cup of coffee and a bag. She doesn't notice Victor's mother. "Here. I brought us some cookies and chips to **share**." Then, she sees Victor's mother. "Oh, hello. Who's this, Victor?"

Iris looks at Lee Ann and says, "And who is this? Victor, what is going on here?"

Reading Comprehension

A Circle *True* or *False*.

1.	Victor was nervous about Vanessa's invitation.	True	False
2.	Vanessa wants to know Victor better.	True	False
3.	Victor is disappointed.	True	False
4.	Victor encourages Vanessa to call him.	True	False
5.	Victor's family thinks he is at work today.	True	False
6.	The study group is working well together.	True	False
7.	Everyone leaves at 12:00.	True	False
8.	Victor plans to leave early.	True	False

B Circle the correct answer.

1. Vanessa thanks Victor for _____.
   a. buying her coffee
   b. tutoring her in math
   c. asking her to join the study group
   d. inviting her to his home

2. Vanessa apologizes to Victor because _____.
   a. she didn't need his help
   b. she didn't know that he was married
   c. she couldn't pay for her snack
   d. he was angry about her invitation

3. When Victor sees his mother, he is _____.
   a. embarrassed and anxious to explain
   b. angry and upset
   c. anxious to go home
   d. happy to see her

4. Victor's mother, Iris, is upset because _____.
   a. Victor didn't invite her to the coffee shop
   b. Victor never calls her
   c. Victor told his father but not her
   d. Victor is at the coffee shop with two women

C Write the names of the characters in the correct sentence. Use one name twice.

Iris	Janet	Lee Ann	Roberto	Vanessa	Victor

1. _____ is going to work today.

2. _____ didn't expect to see Victor at the coffee shop.

3. _____ is a serious and hard teacher.

4. _____ didn't want to meet in a public place.

5. _____ was surprised to hear Victor was married.

6. _____ brought the group a snack.

7. _____ is in trouble with his mother.

Work with the Words

A Circle the correct answer.

1. Keith was **flattered** when _____.
   a. his wife didn't like his suit
   b. his boss told him he was a very hard worker
   c. his children told him that his tie was ugly
   d. a car pulled in front of his car

2. Susan's boyfriend got **jealous** when _____.
   a. she received a letter from an ex-boyfriend
   b. she called him on his cell phone
   c. she gave him a birthday present
   d. she made him a special dinner

3. The children have to **take turns** because _____.
   a. there are two computers
   b. they don't have a computer
   c. there is only one computer in their house
   d. there are many games in their house

4. My teacher is very **tough**. He _____.
   a. never gives homework
   b. gives only one test a year
   c. gives a lot of homework and tests
   d. doesn't give any tests

5. If you miss class, you can ask _____ for the **notes**.
   a. your teacher
   b. another student
   c. another teacher
   d. the principal

6. At 10:30 A.M. I usually have _____ for a **snack**.
   a. coffee and a doughnut
   b. chicken, rice, and broccoli
   c. a hot dog, French fries, and a soda
   d. turkey, vegetables, and a potato

7. Our apartment is very small, so my two daughters **share** _____.
   a. a shirt
   b. shoes
   c. a bedroom
   d. breakfast

8. Andy **asked** Betsy **out**. They went to _____.
   a. the laundromat
   b. the bank
   c. a class
   d. a movie and dinner

B Complete the conversations with the correct words and phrases. You will not use all of the words.

ask him out	jealous	share	take turns
flattered	notes	snack	tough

1. **A:** Mom! I want to play the video game, and Mitch won't let me play.

   B: Mitch, you and your sister have to _____. You can play for five more minutes. Then give it to your sister.

   A: Aw, Mom!

2. **A:** Excuse me, may I see your I.D., please?

   B: My I.D.? I'm _____, young man, but I'm old enough to be your mother.

3. **A:** I'm hungry. Can I have a _____?

   B: Here's an apple.

4. **A:** Did you pass the driving test?

   B: No. That's a _____ test. I failed the parking section.

5. **A:** I really need something to drink.

   B: Here. I have an extra cup. I'll _____ my water with you.

   A: Thanks.

6. **A:** Are you dating Tony?

   B: Not yet. He's a little shy, so I'm going to _____.

7. **A:** Are you _____?

   B: I sure am. I don't like my girlfriend to talk to any other guys.

Lifeskill Practice

Preparing for a test

There are many ways to prepare for a test. Victor and a few of his classmates formed a study group. Here are a few ways to prepare:

1. Make a list and ask a friend to test you.

2. Form a study group and share notes.

3. Review the corrections on your papers.

4. Make flash cards with the English word on one side and your native language on the other.

5. Use a highlighter and highlight the important parts of your textbook.

6. Review your notes and highlight the important parts.

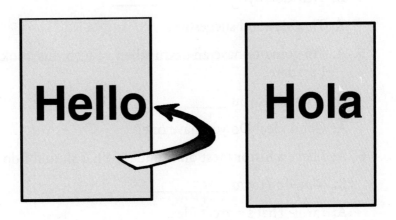

A Complete the conversations. Use the study suggestions on page 73.

1. **A:** I have a vocabulary test this week. How can I prepare for it?

   B: Why don't you _____?

   A: That's a good idea.

2. **A:** I have a big test next week. How should I prepare for it?

   B: Why don't you _____?

   A: Thanks. I'll do that.

3. **A:** I have a spelling test tomorrow. I need help.

   B: Why don't you _____?

   A: That's a good idea. Would you help me?

4. **A:** We have a writing test in two days. How can I prepare for it?

   B: Why don't you _____?

   A: That's a good suggestion.

5. **A:** I'm going to have an exam when I finish this book. How should I prepare?

   B: Why don't you _____?

   A: Good idea! Do you have one?

6. **A:** I have a history test on Monday. What should I do to get ready?

   B: Why don't you _____?

   A: I will. That's a great idea.

B Pairs. Ask your partner for some study suggestions.

Dialogue Practice

Practice the conversation with three classmates.

Vanessa: Thank you for inviting me to join the study group, Victor.

Victor: Not at all, Vanessa.

Vanessa: I really needed help with the math, but you're all helping me with the other subjects, too. I feel much more confident now. I think I can pass the exam.

Victor: Me, too. I really like studying in a group. Everyone has something different to add to the group.

Vanessa: This was your idea, wasn't it?

Victor: Well, actually, Roberto and I both thought it was a good idea. Then we talked to Lee Ann and Janet.

Vanessa: It was a great idea. By the way, I'm sorry about asking you out. I didn't know you were married. I guess you thought I was crazy.

Victor: Well, yeah, a little bit, but that's OK, Vanessa. I was flattered. It's not every day that a young woman like you asks a middle-aged man like me out for coffee.

Iris: VICTOR! WHAT ARE YOU DOING?

Victor: Mom! Uh . . . Hi! What are you doing here?

Iris: What am I doing here? I was having lunch with some friends. What are you doing here with this . . . this woman?

Victor: Mom, this is . . .

Lee Ann: Here. I brought us some cookies and chips to share. Oh, hello. Who's this, Victor?

Iris: And who is this? Victor, what is going on here?

The Secret Is Out!

Get Ready to Read

A **Discuss with a partner.**

1. Why is Victor's mother angry?

2. Why are Vanessa and Lee Ann sitting at a different table from Victor?

3. Do you think Victor will tell his mother about his class?

B **Match the words and expressions with the definitions.**

__f__ 1. fault

_____ 2. switch

_____ 3. ashamed (of)

_____ 4. argue

_____ 5. blame

_____ 6. turn down

_____ 7. stressful

a. embarrassed or guilty

b. say or think someone is responsible for something wrong

c. fight (with words only)

d. refuse an invitation or offer

e. makes you nervous or upset

f. responsibility for a mistake or problem

g. change from one to another

In the last episode...

Victor turns down Vanessa's invitation to have coffee, and he also says that he doesn't have time to tutor her. He invites her to join his study group, and she accepts. A week later, Victor and his study group are at a coffee shop to prepare for their midterm exam. Roberto and Janet have to leave early, but Victor, Lee Ann, and Vanessa continue working. They are taking a short break when Victor's mother, Iris, comes in. When she sees Victor with two women she doesn't know, she gets angry, and now she wants to know what's going on.

⌒ "WHAT'S GOING ON?" shouts Victor's mother.

People at other tables are beginning to look at them. Iris, Victor's mother, is getting excited and is starting to yell at Victor in Portuguese. Lee Ann and Vanessa don't know what to do.

Victor quickly stands up and puts his arm around his mother's shoulder, "Mom, Mom, calm down," he says in Portuguese. His mother stops shouting.

Then, he **switches** back to English. "Mom, this is Lee Ann Waters, and this is Vanessa Baker. They are two of the classmates in my study group," Victor explains.

"A study group? You and two women? What kind of group is that?" asks Iris.

"Mom, please sit down," says Victor.

"Yes, Mrs. Santos," says Lee Ann. "Please, sit here," and Lee Ann pulls out a chair. "Would you like a drink of water? Vanessa, go get a glass of water for Mrs. Santos." Vanessa gets up.

"No, thank you. I'll be fine," Iris says. Vanessa sits back down, but she and Lee Ann are watching Iris carefully. Victor sits down next to his mother.

Lee Ann realizes that Victor needs to talk to his mother alone. "Come on, Vanessa. Let's go. We can finish studying at my house."

Victor stops them. "No, wait. Don't go. I really want to see your notes, Lee Ann, and yours too, Vanessa. Can you wait a few minutes?"

"OK," Lee Ann says, "but we're only going to wait a few minutes. I have somewhere to go later."

Then Vanessa says, "We'll go over there and wait." They go to another table.

"Mom, are you ready to listen to me?" asks Victor.

"Yes, Victor," says Iris. "Now, tell me what's going on, and who are those women? That woman is young enough to be your daughter!"

"I told you, Mom," says Victor. "Lee Ann and Vanessa are in my study group. I'm taking a class, and we have a big exam next week."

"A class? What kind of class? I talked to Marisa yesterday, and she didn't say anything about a class. She said that you were working too much. She's not happy, Victor," says Iris.

"Mom, Marisa doesn't know about my class."

Iris frowns at him. "Marisa doesn't know about your class? Victor, what are you talking about? I'm confused!"

"I'm taking a special class to earn my high school diploma," says Victor.

"Your high school diploma? Oh, Victor . . . " Iris is **speechless**.*

"Marisa doesn't know about the class, and she doesn't know that I don't have a diploma. Nobody knows," says Victor.

"What?" says Iris. "But Victor, it's nothing to be **ashamed of**. You were helping your family. We didn't want you to drop out of school. Do you remember? We **argued** about it for weeks!"

"Of course I remember, Mom," says Victor. "But Dad was so sick. He couldn't work. We needed money. Come on, Mom, don't . . . "

Iris begins to cry. "I'm so sorry, honey. We always thought you could go back later, but you were making money. Dad got better and started working again. We thought you were happy. Of course, we wanted you to get your diploma, but you didn't say anything."

"Mom, don't **blame** yourself. It's not your **fault**. It's my fault. I didn't go back to school after Dad got better. I liked working, but now it's a problem. I didn't get that promotion because I don't have a diploma."

"What?" says Iris.

"That's right. I lied. There isn't a freeze on promotions. The manager found out that I didn't have a diploma."

Iris starts crying again. "Oh, Victor!"

"Mom, calm down. I'm going back now, and I want to keep it a secret. I only have four more weeks of classes. And I'm one of the best students."

"Really? Well, you were an excellent student. That's why we felt so bad when you dropped out."

"Don't worry about that now. We have a bigger problem. You're the only one who knows," says Victor.

"How about your sisters?" asks Iris.

"Are you kidding? Ana can't keep a secret, and Luisa talks to Marisa almost every day. Don't say anything!"

"But what about your father? Can I tell him?"

"OK, you can tell Dad. I know that I can trust him."

"Victor, I am very proud of you." Iris hugs Victor. She starts crying again, but this time, they are happy tears.

---

*speechless = without words; you can't speak because you're very upset, angry, or surprised

"OK, OK, Mom. Your friends are waiting for you over there. Don't say anything to them," says Victor.

"All right. Apologize to your friends for me. I'm so embarrassed. You know I don't like to **make a scene**."*

"I know. I know. I'll call you later," Victor says, and he kisses his mother. Iris goes to join her friends. Victor waves to Vanessa and Lee Ann. They come back to his table.

Lee Ann asks, "Victor, is everything OK? Your mother looked very upset, and you don't look too good either."

Victor points to his mother and her friends talking and laughing.

"See. She's fine." Then Victor says, "I'm OK, Lee Ann. My mother didn't know about this class, so she was upset when she saw me with two strange women."

Lee Ann laughs, "Really? I'm flattered."

Vanessa is more serious. "Victor, why doesn't she know about our class?"

---

*make a scene = bring attention to yourself

Victor looks down at his papers. Then he says, "Well, I'm trying to keep this a secret from my family. Nobody knew before today, but today my mother found out, and now my father will know."

"Why is it a secret, Victor?" asks Vanessa.

"It's complicated, Vanessa. I'll tell everybody when the class is over." "Good luck keeping your secret," says Lee Ann. "Your daughter is in high school, isn't she?"

"Yes, she is, but she's not at school in the evenings. She plays soccer, and the field is not at the school," says Victor.

"Where does your wife think you are every evening?" asks Vanessa.

Victor says, "Everyone thinks that I'm working overtime. But keeping a secret is very **stressful**. I have trouble sleeping, and I know that I get angry easily. I'm glad there are only four more weeks of class."

"Me, too," says Lee Ann. "It's hard to study five nights a week and work full-time."

"**You can say that again**,"*says Victor.

Reading Comprehension

A Circle *True* or *False*.

1.	Iris is very upset when she sees Victor with his friends.	**True**	**False**
2.	Lee Ann is concerned about Iris.	**True**	**False**
3.	Vanessa and Lee Ann decide to go to Lee Ann's house.	**True**	**False**
4.	Iris talks to Marisa about Victor's class.	**True**	**False**
5.	Iris feels sorry that Victor dropped out of school.	**True**	**False**
6.	Iris and Victor's father expected Victor to return to high school.	**True**	**False**
7.	Before today, Iris knew why Victor didn't get the promotion.	**True**	**False**
8.	Iris is going to tell her daughters about Victor's secret.	**True**	**False**

*You can say that again = *I strongly agree with you.*

B Circle the correct answer.

1. Who knows that Victor is going to a special class?
   - **a.** Victor's sisters
   - **b.** Marisa
   - **c.** Iris
   - **d.** Victor's children

2. Iris is _____ to know that Victor is returning to school.
   - **a.** upset
   - **b.** proud and happy
   - **c.** sad and guilty
   - **d.** not interested

3. Iris is embarrassed because _____.
   - **a.** Lee Ann and Vanessa are leaving the coffee shop
   - **b.** Victor doesn't have a diploma
   - **c.** Victor is angry with her
   - **d.** other customers are looking at her

4. When Lee Ann and Vanessa come back to the table, they're worried about _____.
   - **a.** Victor and Iris
   - **b.** the study group
   - **c.** Victor
   - **d.** Victor's family

C Answer the questions.

1. Why did Lee Ann want to get some water for Iris?

   _____

2. Why didn't Victor go back to school when his father started working again?

   _____

3. Why is Victor having trouble sleeping?

   _____

4. What is difficult for Lee Ann and Victor?

   _____

Work with the Words

A Circle the correct answer.

1. I **turned down** _____ because I had to work.
   - **a.** a promotion
   - **b.** the bed
   - **c.** an invitation to a party
   - **d.** a book

2. The student wanted to **switch** _____ because the schoolwork was too easy.
   - **a.** principals
   - **b.** pencils
   - **c.** cars
   - **d.** classes

3. After John's parents talked to his teacher, they were **ashamed of** John's _____.
   - **a.** bad behavior
   - **b.** good grades
   - **c.** high test scores
   - **d.** many friends

4. The children didn't want to _____, so they started to **argue**.
   - **a.** have fun
   - **b.** share the game
   - **c.** enjoy the party
   - **d.** open the presents

5. When my brother broke our mother's favorite vase, he **blamed** _____.
   - **a.** our mother
   - **b.** the vase
   - **c.** the dog
   - **d.** the neighbor

6. When the police officer came, I told her that the _____ wasn't my **fault**.
   - **a.** car
   - **b.** driver
   - **c.** accident
   - **d.** traffic

7. It is very **stressful** to _____.
   - **a.** drive on a quiet road
   - **b.** drive in heavy traffic
   - **c.** receive presents
   - **d.** have a nice dinner with your family

8. Mr. Jones was **speechless** when _____.
   - **a.** he forgot his speech
   - **b.** he had a lot to say to the audience
   - **c.** he saw his damaged car
   - **d.** he remembered what he wanted to say

B Match each word or phrase with its opposite.

_____ 1. turn down   **a.** not change

_____ 2. switch   **b.** get along

_____ 3. speechless   **c.** relaxing

_____ 4. ashamed   **d.** accept

_____ 5. argue   **e.** talkative

_____ 6. stressful   **f.** proud

C Complete the conversations with the correct words and phrases. You will not use all of the words.

ashamed	blamed	fault	make a scene	turned down

1. There was an accident on the corner between a large truck and a very small car. Mr. Banks, who was driving the truck, __blamed__ the driver of the small car, a 90-year-old man, Mr. Jones. Mr. Banks said, "It's his __fault__! He's too old to drive." When the ambulance came, Mr. Jones __turned down__ medical treatment because he didn't want to __make a scene__. He just wanted to go home.

argued	references	speechless	stressful	switch

2. The Benjamins are going to move to a new neighborhood. Moving is very __stressful__, especially for children. The children don't want to __switch__ schools in the middle of the school year, so last night they __argued__ with their parents about the move. They want to live with their friends until the end of the school year.

Lifeskill Practice

We use *would you like* to offer something to eat or drink, or to offer an invitation.

A Practice the conversations with a partner.

1. **A:** **Would you like** something to eat?
   B: No, thank you.

2. **A:** **Would you like** something to drink?
   B: Yes, please.
   A: What would you like?
   B: I'll have some hot tea, please.

3. **A:** **Would you like** to go to the movies?
   B: Yes, I would.
   A: What would you like to see?
   B: I'd like to see an action movie.

B Complete the conversations with a partner. Use your imagination.

1. **A:** **Would you like** something to eat?
   B: _____.

2. **A:** **Would you like** something to drink?
   B: Yes, please.
   A: What would you like?
   B: I'll have _____, please.

3. **A:** **Would you like** to go to _____?
   B: Yes, I would.
   A: _____ would you like to _____?
   B: I'd like to _____.

Dialogue Practice

Practice the conversation with three classmates.

Iris: WHAT'S GOING ON?

Victor: Mom, Mom, calm down. Mom, this is Lee Ann Waters, and this is Vanessa Baker. They are two of my classmates in my study group.

Iris: A study group? You and two women? What kind of group is that?

Victor: Mom, please sit down.

Lee Ann: Yes, Mrs. Santos. Please, sit here. Would you like a drink of water? Vanessa, go get a glass of water for Mrs. Santos.

Iris: No, thank you. I'll be fine.

Lee Ann: Come on, Vanessa. Let's go. We can finish studying at my house.

Victor: No, wait. Don't go. I really want to see your notes, Lee Ann, and yours too, Vanessa. Can you wait a few minutes?

Lee Ann: OK, but we're only going to wait a few minutes. I have somewhere to go later.

Vanessa : We'll go over there and wait.

Not Again!

Episode

9

Get Ready to Read

A Discuss with a partner.

1. Why do you think Marisa is angry?
2. What is Victor going to say to her?
3. What is Marisa going to say to Victor?

B Match the words and expressions with the definitions.

_d_ 1. (have) a temperature

_____ 2. worth it

_____ 3. from now on

_____ 4. anniversary

_____ 5. dead (battery; power)

_____ 6. rehearsal

_____ 7. strict

a. practice, usually for a performance

b. tough; expect someone to follow rules

c. not working

d. have a fever

e. useful or helpful

f. starting today; going into the future

g. yearly celebration of a marriage or other event

In the last episode...

Victor is at a coffee shop studying with two members of his study group, Lee Ann and Vanessa. Suddenly, Victor's mother, Iris, arrives at the shop with some friends. She sees Victor with two strange women and gets angry. When she finally calms down, Victor has to tell her about the class. Iris is very proud of her son and promises not to say anything to Marisa or to his sisters. Victor gives her permission to tell his father.

🎧 Marisa is waiting in the kitchen for Victor to come home. Jordan is sleeping, and Alex is out with friends. It's about four o'clock, and Victor is late. He told Marisa that he was going to be home by one o'clock. Marisa is angry. Then Fred starts barking.

Victor walks in the back door. He's in a great mood. "Hey, Marisa! I'm home! Hey, Fred! How are you doing?" Fred is jumping on Victor.

"Shh. Jordan's sleeping. So, you're finally home."

Victor stops smiling, "Jordan's sleeping? At four o'clock in the afternoon? Is something wrong?"

Marisa is frowning. She looks like she's going to scream. "Is something wrong? Is something wrong? Let me tell you about my great day. I worked at the office from 8:30 to 12:00 because there was a mistake at work. I picked up Jordan from his baseball game. His team won, but you weren't there again. Then we drove to the library to pick up Alex. She needed some help on a project, so we stayed for another hour. Then we picked up lunch on the way home. When we got home, Jordan **threw up*** all over the kitchen floor. He had a **temperature**, so I put him to bed. Then I cleaned up and walked Fred. Oh, I had a great day!!"

Victor stops smiling and is very careful about what he says next. "Marisa, honey, I'm sorry. I'm sorry that I wasn't there to help you. I'm sorry that I missed Jordan's game. The project will finish in only four more weeks, and then . . . "

Marisa interrupts, "Four more weeks? Four more WEEKS? You said that you had to work today, but this is too much. You're out late every night, and you're out on Saturdays, too. When you're home, you're in the office with the door

***threw up** = vomited

closed. Talk to your boss, Victor. Maybe you can take a few nights off. We never see you anymore. I hope all of this extra work is **worth it**. I hope your bosses see how hard you're working."

Victor thinks about it, and then he answers. "Marisa, sweetie. Listen. I'm only doing this for our family. I can't take time off, but I promise this extra work will be worth it. You'll see. But I will try to come home earlier **from now on**. And, this Saturday, we can do something special."

Marisa calms down and stops frowning. "Something special? That would be nice. Maybe we can go out to dinner and take the kids to a movie."

"I have a better idea. **Instead*** you and I can go on a date, just the two of us. Do you remember that French restaurant that I took you to last year?"

"Of course, I do. It was our **anniversary**," says Marisa.

"Well, why don't I take you there again?"

"What about Jordan? Maybe Alex can babysit."

Victor thinks for a moment, and says, "Alex is usually out with her friends on Saturday nights. I'll call Luisa and ask if she can babysit. They always have fun."

Marisa is smiling. "Really? That would be wonderful."

Victor hugs and kisses Marisa. "OK, it's a date. Saturday night. Just you and me."

*   *   *   *

It's Friday night a week later. As usual, Victor and his study group are getting together after class to review and to help each other with their homework.

It's about 8:30 when Victor and his study group stop working. They all decide to take a break and meet tomorrow. They will meet in the afternoon because Victor wants to go to Jordan's baseball game in the morning.

Victor is standing in front of the building talking to one of the other students when he sees Vanessa get out of her car. She walks around to the front of her car and opens the **hood**.** She's looking under the hood, but she doesn't know what to do. Victor says to his friend, "Roberto, it looks like Vanessa is having some car trouble. Why don't you give her some help?"

Robert replies, "Are you kidding? I don't even own a car. I'm waiting for my brother to pick me up."

***instead** = in the place of something

****hood** = metal cover over the engine of a car, usually in the front of the car

"I guess I'll go help her," Victor says and walks across the street.

"Vanessa, what's wrong?" Victor asks.

"My car won't start. I think I accidentally left my lights on. Can you help me?" she asks.

"Sure. Your battery's **dead**. I'll get my cables and give you a jump start."

"Thanks a lot, Victor. You're a lifesaver."

A few minutes later, Vanessa's car is working again. Victor is wiping his hands on his pants. "Wait a minute, Victor," Vanessa says. "I'll get you something to clean your hands."

Vanessa is looking in her purse when suddenly Victor hears, "Dad, Dad!"

Victor looks up to see his daughter, Alex, running across from the school. At first, she is happy to see him, but when she sees Vanessa, she starts frowning. Victor thinks to himself, "Not again! First my mother, and now Alex. What am I going to do?"

"What are you doing here, and who is that?" says Alex, pointing to Vanessa.

At first, Victor doesn't know what to say. "Um, uh. What are you doing at school so late?"

"I asked you first," she replies. "Anyway, I had a late **rehearsal** for the play. We were practicing some changes in the dances. Answer my question."

Vanessa interrupts, "Victor, is this your daughter? Hi, my name's Vanessa. I'm one of your father's classmates."

"A classmate?" Alex says. "What class?"

Victor immediately grabs his daughter and walks away. "Bye, Vanessa."

"Dad, what is she talking about?" Alex asks. She's standing with her hands on her hips, looking just like her mother.

Victor sighs, "All right, all right. Alex, I was trying to keep a secret."

Alex gets excited, "A secret? Is it something to do with me? Is it a present?"

Victor says, "No, no, Alex. It's not a present."

Alex asks, "Are you sure? Is it a car? That's it, isn't it? You're giving me a car for my graduation!"

"No, it's not a car. Listen to me, Alex. I'm trying to do something for our family. It was a secret from all of you, but now it's going to be a secret between you, me, and your grandparents."

Victor tells Alex everything. In the beginning, she frowns, trying to understand. Then she begins to smile.

Victor is confused, "What are you smiling about? Aren't you disappointed in me? I have always been very **strict** with you kids about school. I always tell you that education is important for your future."

"But Dad, how can I be disappointed? This is the best news! I'm so proud of you." Alex hugs her father, which almost makes him cry. "I can't wait to see Mom's face when she finds out!"

"Remember, Alex. Don't say a word to anyone. I have only three more weeks."

"I promise," she says. "I won't say a word."

Reading Comprehension

A Circle *True* or *False*.

1.	Marisa was waiting to have lunch with Victor.	True	False
2.	Marisa had a bad day.	True	False
3.	Jordan is sleeping because he is tired.	True	False
4.	Victor is going to take Marisa out next weekend.	True	False
5.	The study group will meet again tomorrow.	True	False
6.	Vanessa knows how to fix a car.	True	False
7.	Roberto and Victor help Vanessa.	True	False
8.	Victor's hands are dirty after he helps Vanessa.	True	False

B Circle the correct answer.

1. Why didn't Vanessa's car start?
   a. It was out of gas.
   b. The battery was dead.
   c. She had an accident.
   d. The battery was missing.

2. Why did Alex frown when she saw Vanessa?
   a. She was angry at her father.
   b. She knew her and didn't like her.
   c. She was too busy to talk to her.
   d. She was surprised to see her talking to her father.

3. When Alex hears about a secret, she thinks _____.
   a. her father's going to take her out to dinner
   b. her father is having a relationship with Vanessa
   c. her father is in trouble
   d. she's going to get a new car

C Put the sentences in order from 1 to 8.

_____ a. Marisa had to clean the kitchen floor.

_____ b. Marisa picked up food for lunch.

_____ c. Marisa helped Alex with her project.

_____ d. Marisa left work.

_____ e. Victor got home late.

_____ f. Jordan threw up.

_____ g. Victor promised to take Marisa on a date.

_____ h. Marisa waited for Victor in the kitchen.

Work with the Words

Ⓐ **Circle the correct answer.**

1. I took the baby _____ because she had a **temperature** for a few hours.
   - **a.** to the beach
   - **b.** to the supermarket
   - **c.** to the doctor
   - **d.** to work

2. The student hopes that all of his _____ is **worth it**.
   - **a.** eating
   - **b.** partying
   - **c.** talking
   - **d.** studying

3. **Police officer:** I'm giving you a warning. Watch the speed limit.

   Driver: I promise, Officer. **From now on,** _____.
   - **a.** I'll go faster
   - **b.** I'll drive too slowly
   - **c.** I'll pay attention
   - **d.** I'm sorry

4. For their **anniversary**, Bob and his wife want to _____.
   - **a.** get a birthday cake
   - **b.** clean the house
   - **c.** go out to dinner
   - **d.** go to the supermarket

5. The cell phone batteries are **dead**, so I _____.
   - **a.** can't make any calls
   - **b.** can call long distance
   - **c.** can call locally
   - **d.** can only talk a short time

6. Who goes to **rehearsals**?
   - **a.** professional singers
   - **b.** doctors
   - **c.** football players
   - **d.** high school teachers

7. A **strict** teacher _____.
   - **a.** doesn't give any homework
   - **b.** gives homework every day
   - **c.** doesn't care what the students do
   - **d.** gives the students candy

8. I don't want to go out for dinner. **Instead,** let's _____.
   - **a.** go to a fast food restaurant
   - **b.** eat at the mall
   - **c.** eat at that new Mexican café
   - **d.** call and order a pizza

B Complete the sentences. Use the words in the box. You do not
need all of the words.

anniversary	dead	instead	strict
a temperature	from now on	rehearsal	worth it

1. Victor thinks that all of the late studying will be _____
   to his family. Marisa wants him to be home more. Victor promises
   that _____ he will try to come home earlier.

2. The student orchestra usually has a _____ on Tuesday
   night. This week the teacher couldn't come because he was
   celebrating his wedding _____, so we met on
   Wednesday night _____.

Lifeskill Practice

■ It's useful to know the names of important parts of a car.

A Write the names of the parts of a car next to the numbers.

accelerator	hood	steering wheel	trunk
brake	seatbelt	tire	windshield

1. _____   5. _____

2. _____   6. _____

3. _____   7. _____

4. _____   8. _____

B Practice the conversations with a partner. Take turns.

1. **A:** What should I do first?
   B: First, put on your seatbelt. Then look in the rearview mirror.

2. **A:** What should I do when the light turns green?
   B: Take your foot off the brake and step on the accelerator.

3. **A:** Where is the spare tire?
   B: It's in the trunk.

4. **A:** Why isn't the car working?
   B: I don't know. Look under the hood.

Dialogue Practice

Practice the conversation with two classmates. Act it out.

Alex: What are you doing here, and who is that?

Victor: Um, uh. What are you doing at school so late?

Alex: I asked you first. Anyway, I had a late rehearsal for the play. We were practicing some changes in the dances. Answer my question.

Vanessa: Victor, is this your daughter? Hi, my name's Vanessa. I'm one of your father's classmates.

Alex: A classmate? What class?

Victor: Bye, Vanessa.

Alex: Dad, what is she talking about?

Victor: All right, all right. Alex, I was trying to keep a secret.

Alex: A secret? Is it something to do with me? Is it a present?

Victor: No, no, Alex. It's not a present.

Alex: Are you sure? Is it a car? That's it, isn't it? You're giving me a car for my graduation!

Victor: No, it's not a car. Listen to me, Alex. I'm trying to do something for our family. It was a secret from all of you, but now it's going to be a secret between you, me, and your grandparents.

A Late Date

Get Ready to Read

A Discuss with a partner.

1. Who is going out tonight?
2. Where are they going?
3. When do you think Marisa is going to learn the truth about Victor's secret?

B Match the words and expressions with the definitions.

  _e_   **1.** drop off   **a.** grade point average

  _____   **2.** occasion   **b.** very nervous and worried

  _____   **3.** impressed   **c.** a special event

  _____   **4.** frantic   **d.** think something is good

  _____   **5.** arrest   **e.** take someone or something somewhere

  _____   **6.** GPA   **f.** to make noise, usually because of something good

  _____   **7.** cheer

           g. police take a person to the police station

In the last episode...

Victor comes home late from his study group, and Marisa is angry. She complains that the family never sees him anymore. Victor promises to come home earlier from now on and also promises to take Marisa out next Saturday for a special evening.

The following Friday evening, Victor and his study group finish early. Vanessa has trouble with her car, and Victor helps her. Just when he is about to leave, Alex appears. He has to tell her his secret, and he makes her promise not to tell anyone.

🎧 It's Saturday morning, and before Victor leaves the house, he promises to be home by seven o'clock for his date with Marisa. He and his study group are meeting at 3:30 so that Victor can go to Jordan's baseball game. Victor calls, "Jordan! Come on! We're going to be late!"

"I'm coming!" yells Jordan.

"OK, I'll be home by seven o'clock," says Victor.

After the game, Victor **drops off** Jordan at home. Then he goes to meet his friends at the high school. Because Alex knows about his class, he isn't worried about seeing her at the high school.

Later that evening, Marisa is getting dressed up for her date. She's excited about this special **occasion**. She's not worried about the time because Victor promised to be home by seven o'clock.

Alex is visiting a friend, so Victor's sister, Luisa, is going to stay with Jordan. The doorbell rings, and Jordan runs downstairs. "I'll get it! I'll get it!"

It's Luisa. "Hi, Aunt Lu! We're going to have fun tonight!"

"We sure are, Jordan! I brought a few DVDs, a new video game, and some popcorn."

"Great!" Marisa comes downstairs. She looks beautiful.

"Wow, Mom! You're beautiful! Dad will be really **impressed**."

"I hope so," says Marisa. "What time is it?"

Luisa looks at her watch. "It's only 6:45. Relax. He'll be here."

"I'm just a little nervous. The last time just the two of us went out together was our anniversary last year. Now I feel like a teenager again." Marisa's smiling.

Thirty minutes later, Marisa is still waiting. Then the phone rings. She picks up the phone.

"Victor? Where are you?"

"Mom, it's me."

"Alex, what's wrong?" asks Marisa.

"Can you pick me up at school?"

"What are you doing at school? I thought you were at Angela's house."

"Angela and I are here to practice for the play, but she's not feeling well, and her parents aren't home. Can you pick us up?"

"OK," says Marisa, "Your father's late anyway. Aunt Lu can stay with Jordan. I'll be there in ten minutes."

Marisa yells to Luisa and Jordan, "Lu, I'm going to the high school to pick up Alex. When Victor gets home, tell him I'll be right back."

About ten minutes later, Marisa parks in front of the school. The door of the school opens and Marisa looks over, expecting to see Alex. Instead, she sees Victor and a very young, attractive woman. The woman is smiling at Victor. Marisa is shocked. "Who is that?" Marisa wonders to herself. She doesn't know that Victor and Vanessa are classmates, and she doesn't see his friends. She immediately **misunderstands*** and thinks, "All this time, Victor said that he was working overtime. He lied. He's with . . . he's with . . . another woman!" She begins to cry, and she gets ready to drive away.

Alex comes out of the high school. She is surprised to see her father. "Dad, why aren't you at home getting ready? Look, there's Mom! She looks upset. What's wrong?" Victor sees Marisa. He looks at Vanessa and realizes that Marisa saw her and has the wrong idea. He runs across the street to stop her, with Alex running behind him.

"Dad, what's wrong? Why is Mom leaving?"

Marisa drives off. Victor can see her crying. Victor yells, "Marisa! Marisa! Wait!" Then, suddenly, he sees a truck speeding down the street. "Look out!"

Marisa pulls to the right and misses the truck. She hits a tree, and the truck hits three parked cars before it stops. Victor and Alex are **frantic**.

*misunderstands = get the wrong idea

"OH, NO! OH, NO! Marisa! Marisa!" Victor runs to Marisa's van. Alex is right behind him. Fortunately, Marisa was wearing her seatbelt. Her eyes are closed. "Marisa! Marisa! Are you all right?" Victor shouts. "Someone call 911!"

Victor's classmates are standing around the car. Vanessa gets out her cell phone and dials 911.

Alex is crying, "Mom, Mom! Wake up! Dad! What's wrong with her? Is she hurt?"

Victor has tears in his eyes. He touches Marisa's face. "Honey, please wake up. It's me, Victor. Everything's going to be fine, honey. Wake up."

Slowly, Marisa opens her eyes. She looks at Victor's face. "Wha . . . Wha . . . What happened?"

Victor and Alex are relieved. "Oh, thank goodness, you're all right." Victor and Alex hug each other.

Victor's classmates are standing nearby. Lee Ann says to Marisa, "Don't move. You had an accident. The police are coming."

"Where am I?" Marisa asks Victor.

"You're near the high school. Remember? A truck was out of control. You hit a tree. Are you OK?"

Marisa moves a little bit. "I . . . I think so." She feels her arms and legs, but she can't get out of the car. "I don't think I broke anything."

Victor looks at her and holds her hand. "Just stay still. Don't move."

Marisa looks at Alex, and then she looks outside at all the people. Then, she sees Vanessa standing on the sidewalk. Vanessa looks worried. Marisa remembers what happened. She begins to frown. "Victor, who is that woman?"

Alex laughs, "Don't worry, Mom. That's Vanessa, one of Dad's classmates."

Marisa says, "Classmates?"

Victor says, "It's a long story, Marisa, but first, let me tell you this. There is nothing going on between me and Vanessa. You misunderstood. All of us are in a class together. Now, try to relax. I think I hear the ambulance."

A police car and an ambulance arrive.

"I'll explain everything later." Victor waves to the ambulance.

The emergency medical technicians (EMTs) get out of the ambulance and carefully check Marisa. Then they put her on a **stretcher*** to carry her to the ambulance. The police are talking to the truck driver. They are going to **arrest** him for speeding. They will question Marisa later. Victor gets into the ambulance with Marisa. Roberto drives Vanessa to the hospital.

On the way to the hospital, Marisa makes Victor tell her everything. Marisa looks at Victor and asks, "Victor, why didn't you tell me? We've been married for almost twenty years! Why did you keep that secret from me . . . and from your children?"

Victor looks away from Marisa. "I wanted to tell you many times, but I couldn't. I'm sorry. This accident is my fault. I was too ashamed to tell you. After I lost the promotion, I decided to go back to school, but I didn't know if I could do it. Now, I know that I can. I have two more weeks to get my diploma. I'm doing this for you, for Alex, for Jordan, and for me—for our family."

Marisa is crying and Victor becomes scared, "Marisa, are you in pain?"

"No, Victor. I'm proud of you."

"Proud? You're proud of me? How can you be proud of me after what happened? This is my fault," says Victor.

Marisa smiles, "No. It's the truck driver's fault. I'm proud of you, Victor. I know that it was difficult for you to tell me the truth. And don't forget. You promised to take me to that French restaurant."

Two weeks later, everyone is at the high school for graduation. Alex is sitting in the front row with her classmates, dressed in a blue cap and gown. The tassel on her cap is gold because she is a member of the National Honor Society and is one of the top students. Victor has his video camera, and Jordan is taking photos. All of Marisa's and Victor's family is there. It's a happy day.

---

*stretcher = a covered frame for carrying someone who is too injured to walk

Each student is receiving a diploma. The principal says, "With a 3.9 **GPA** and a full scholarship to New Jersey State University, Alexandra Santos!" Victor, Marisa, and the whole family begin to **cheer**. Alexandra walks onto the stage to get her diploma. She smiles and waves at her family.

After all of the students receive their diplomas, the principal walks to the microphone. "May I have your attention, please? We have one more graduate. Mr. Victor Santos, could you come up to the stage, please?"

Victor looks at his family. "What's going on?"

Marisa pushes him out of his chair. "Go up there, honey. We have a surprise for you."

Victor walks up to the stage. Then he sees Ms. Rogers, the teacher from his class. The principal speaks to the audience, "Ladies and gentlemen, today is a very special day. Today, we have two graduates from the same family: Alexandra and Victor Santos! Mr. Santos, congratulations for your excellent work. You graduated with special honors from our Second Chance program. Here's your diploma!" Ms. Rogers shakes Victor's hand and hands him his diploma.

The audience applauds loudly. Victor's sisters are crying, Marisa is crying, and Victor's parents are crying, too. Iris is crying the loudest. It's a wonderful graduation.

Reading Comprehension

A Circle *True* or *False*.

1. Victor cancels his study group meeting.	True	False
2. Victor finally attends Jordan's baseball game.	True	False
3. Victor and Marisa planned a special evening together.	True	False
4. Alex is going to babysit tonight.	True	False
5. Marisa has the wrong idea about Vanessa and Victor.	True	False
6. Marisa breaks her leg.	True	False
7. The police arrest the truck driver.	True	False
8. The police immediately ask Marisa about the accident.	True	False

B Circle the correct answer.

1. Why did Alex need a ride home?

   a. because she was sick **c.** because she couldn't drive

   b. because her friend was sick **d.** because it was very late

2. Who does Marisa see first at the high school?

   a. Alex **c.** Victor and Vanessa

   b. Victor **d.** Jordan

3. Marisa is _____ when she sees Victor with Vanessa.

   a. nervous **c.** angry

   b. excited **d.** disappointed

4. Why do the police arrest the truck driver?

   a. because he was driving too fast

   b. because he didn't stop at a stop sign

   c. because he was talking on his cell phone

   d. because he didn't have a license

C Who is it? Write the names of the characters in the spaces. You will use some names more than once.

Alex	Luisa	Ms. Rogers	Victor
Jordan	Marisa	The study group	

1. _____ is going to stay with Jordan.

2. _____ plans a special evening with his wife.

3. _____ gets together to review class material.

4. _____ teaches a Second Chance class.

5. _____ wants to get a high school diploma.

6. _____ plays baseball.

7. _____ graduates at the top of her class.

8. _____ surprises her father.

9. _____ doesn't know that Vanessa is Victor's classmate.

10. _____ plays soccer.

Work with the Words

A Circle the correct answer.

1. I **drop off** my mail at _____.
   - **a.** my house
   - **b.** the post office
   - **c.** the bank
   - **d.** the supermarket

2. _____ is a special **occasion**.
   - **a.** An exam
   - **b.** The fourth day of school
   - **c.** A 50th wedding anniversary
   - **d.** A doctor's visit

3. When the employee _____, his supervisor was **impressed**.
   - **a.** arrived thirty minutes late
   - **b.** finished the work early
   - **c.** took a long break
   - **d.** didn't come to work

4. The mother became **frantic** when her child _____.
   - **a.** said her first word
   - **b.** took a nap
   - **c.** ate her lunch
   - **d.** got a high fever

5. _____ **arrest** people who break the law.
   - **a.** The police
   - **b.** Teachers
   - **c.** Students
   - **d.** Mothers

6. Because Alex has a high **GPA**, she can _____.
   - **a.** not graduate
   - **b.** graduate with honors
   - **c.** repeat her senior year
   - **d.** not go to college

7. Everyone **cheered** because the team _____.
   - **a.** lost the game
   - **b.** couldn't play
   - **c.** had many missing players
   - **d.** won the game

8. When Marisa saw Victor talking to Vanessa, she **misunderstood**. Circle the sentence with the same meaning.
   - **a.** She jumped into the car.
   - **b.** She became angry.
   - **c.** She didn't understand the situation and made a mistake.
   - **d.** She clearly understood the situation.

B Complete the sentences with the correct words and phrases. You will not use all the words.

apologizes	finds out	instead	relieved
confront	impressed	jealous	unfortunately
drops off	improve	occasion	wonders

1. Marisa _____ why Victor is late. Tonight is a special _____ for them, and Jordan thinks his father will be _____ when he sees Marisa.

2. When Marisa arrives at the high school, she is _____ because Victor is talking to Vanessa. She does not park the car. _____, she quickly drives away. _____, a truck driver appears and causes a serious accident.

3. Marisa is _____ when she _____ the truth. She's happy that Victor wants to _____ his family's life. Victor _____ for not telling her the truth.

Lifeskill Practice

Use 911 to call the police when you have an emergency (fire, medical emergency, dangerous situation).

Practice the conversations with a partner.

1. **A:** 911. What's your emergency?
   B: There's a fire in my house.
   A: Is there anyone in the house?
   B: Yes, my children and our cat.
   A: Can you get everyone out of the house?
   B: I think so.
   A: I have your address. The fire department is on its way. Get out of the house and wait outside.
   B: Thank you.

2. **A:** 911. What is the address of the emergency?
   B: 933 Third Street. It's the Fish Fry Restaurant.
   A: What's the emergency?
   B: A customer passed out. I think he had a heart attack.
   A: Is he breathing?
   B: Yes, but it's very soft.
   A: How old is he?
   B: He's 70. His wife is with him. She said he had a heart attack last year.
   A: Does anyone know **CPR**?*
   B: Yes, one of the waiters is doing CPR on him now.
   A: Good. Someone is on the way.
   B: Thank you.

*CPR (someone) = (cardiopulmonary resuscitation) = a medical procedure to help someone start breathing again

Dialogue Practice

Practice the conversations with two classmates.

Jordan: I'll get it! I'll get it! Hi, Aunt Lu! We're going to have fun tonight!

Lu: We sure are, Jordan. I brought a few DVDs, a new video game, and some popcorn.

Jordan: Great! (Marisa comes downstairs. She looks beautiful.)

Jordan: Wow, Mom! You're beautiful! Dad will be really impressed.

Marisa: I hope so. What time is it?

Lu: It's only 6:45. Relax. He'll be here.

Marisa: I'm just a little nervous. The last time just the two of us went out together was our anniversary last year. Now I feel like a teenager again.

* * * *

Victor: OH, NO! OH, NO! Marisa! Marisa! Marisa! Marisa! Are you all right? Someone call 911!

Alex: (crying) Mom, Mom! Wake up! Dad! What's wrong with her? Is she hurt?

Victor: Honey, please wake up. It's me, Victor. Everything's going to be fine, honey. Wake up.

Marisa: Wha . . . Wha . . . What happened?

Victor: Oh, thank goodness, you're all right.

Lee Ann: Don't move. You had an accident. The police are coming.

Marisa: Where am I?

Victor: You're near the high school. Remember? A truck was out of control. You hit a tree. Are you OK?

Marisa: I . . . I think so. I don't think I broke anything.

Victor: Just stay still. And don't move.